REDEFINING SUCCESS

REDEFINING SUCCESS

FOR A HAPPIER, MORE AUTHENTIC & FULFILLING LIFE

ALISON WOLK CAMPBELL

REDEFINING SUCCESS FOR A HAPPIER,
MORE AUTHENTIC & FULFILLING LIFE

Published by
Martian Goose Publishing
Santa Monica, CA

Copyright © 2020 by Alison Wolk Campbell

Throughout this book, I have drawn on examples from my life as well as from clients, friends, and family members. In some instances, I have changed their names and identifying characteristics to protect their privacy and ensure confidentiality.

Cover design by Michelle Fairbanks, Fresh Design
Book design by JetLaunch
Editing by Maya Lang
Copyediting by Hilary Roberts
Author photograph by Amy Williams

Library of Congress Control Number: 2020904031

Publisher's Cataloging-In-Publication Data
(Prepared by The Donohue Group, Inc.)

Names: Campbell, Alison Wolk, author.
Title: Redefining success for a happier, more authentic & fulfilling life / Alison Wolk Campbell.
Description: [Santa Monica, California] : [Martian Goose Publishing], [2020]
Identifiers: ISBN 9781641842969 | ISBN 9781641842976 (ebook)
Subjects: LCSH: Success--Psychological aspects. | Goal (Psychology) | Self-actualization (Psychology) | Stress management. | Happiness.
Classification: LCC BF637.S8 C36 2020 (print) | LCC BF637.S8 (ebook) | DDC 158.1--dc23

To my husband for his unwavering commitment to being a loving and supportive husband, partner, and father, and for both supporting and joining me in my learning journey. To my children who bring me endless joy and constantly stretch my capacity as a human being. To my parents for their unconditional love, friendship, and unending willingness to step in and help at a moment's notice.

—※—

Do not walk through time without leaving worthy evidence of your passage.

—Pope John XXIII

—※—

CONTENTS

PREFACE

It was 2011. My life was amazing…on paper. Someone observing from the outside would have assumed I had it all. I was happily married to a wonderful and supportive man. We had a healthy and delightful three-year-old son and lived in a house mere blocks from the beach in Santa Monica, California. I had an exciting and challenging job with smart colleagues who were great team players. For an Angeleno, I was unusually lucky: my job was just ten minutes from home. My parents lived nearby, and we enjoyed a warm, open relationship.

Throughout my life, I had done everything expected of me to get to this impressive point. I had gone to an Ivy League university and then earned my MBA from a prestigious program. Over the course of my career, I had held well-respected jobs, earning six-figure salaries at hip, brand-name companies. But beneath it all, I felt like a fraud and a failure. I had one narrow definition of success, and it was making me miserable.

I had always defined success as "making it" in my career. This meant working at a reputable company, receiving recognition for a job well done, and advancing in title and salary. When I became successful according to this definition, I thought, then I would be happy. I'd feel confident and be able to enjoy life. But the way my life was unfolding was not measuring up to my expectations. I was giving it my all at work, only to feel unappreciated and unsupported. My joy and sense of purpose were withering while my feelings of self-doubt and fear flourished like weeds in a garden.

I felt utterly overextended trying to juggle career and motherhood. I wanted to shine at work. I also wanted to shine at home as a hands-on mother to my precious little Cooper.

Becoming a parent opened up a whole new dimension of my life, but I didn't have a specialized degree or any experience when it came to being a mom. I was terrified of doing it wrong. I wanted to raise a kind, well-behaved, thoughtful, and considerate human being. But I had no mentor or manager to supervise my performance, and no metrics to tell me whether I was doing a good job. I felt paralyzed when it came to knowing the right things to say and do. I was afraid I might be a weak parent who let her child run the show. At the top of my list of fears was that I would turn my son into a spoiled brat.

I couldn't figure out what it even meant to be a good mother. Was it how much time I spent with my child?

How actively engaged I was when we were together? How much I enjoyed being with him? What if I preferred talking to other mothers at the park to sitting down in the sandbox and shaping gritty, germ-infused particles into hamburgers? How could I ever know if I was doing it right, or doing enough? These questions consumed me.

Because I was burning the candle at both ends, I figured the solution was to give up activities that weren't related to my job or my family. This felt logical: removing things from my plate would surely make my life easier. However, I didn't anticipate the personal and spiritual costs. As I stopped reading books, going to yoga classes, and getting together with friends, I let go of interests and relationships that had always enlivened me. I laser-focused my time and energy in an effort to accomplish every task on my list, thinking this was the path to the success I so craved.

Then one weekend morning just before the Christmas holiday, we went out as a family to squeeze in some holiday shopping at our local mall before Cooper's nap. Before returning home, we hurried over to the customer service desk. Our preschool had arranged for the mall to donate a small percentage of purchases to the school. As I handed my receipt to the agent, he beamed with holiday cheer. "How's your day going?" he asked warmly.

I paused. It was such an innocent question, but he asked it with such sincerity that I found myself disconcerted by his good cheer. We were both in the same crowded mall, with its too-loud holiday music and throngs of harried shoppers, yet his attitude was vastly different from my own. How do people fake being happy at their jobs? I found myself wondering. I forced myself to return his smile and thank him when he handed back my receipt, but I couldn't shake the moment—the contrast between us.

As we made our way back to the parking structure, it dawned on me that I wasn't being the type of person I wanted to be. My historically positive and upbeat attitude had been replaced by cynicism and hopelessness. It was as though I had reached some foregone conclusion that deriving enjoyment from work was an unrealistic expectation. The heaviness in my heart even blocked me from the one thing I'd always been able to count on to lift my mood—human connection. Someone else's cheerfulness shouldn't throw me for such a loop, nor should my assumption have been that he was faking it. I suddenly realized that I had veered far off course from the life I desired.

I saw that I needed to make a change. It was hard to imagine walking away from my career—the bedrock of my identity and self-worth—and it seemed crazy to give up my income. Yet I couldn't shake my conviction that I was done living this way, burnt out and miserable.

This is when my journey began—not just into a new life but into a new understanding of who I am and how I measure self-worth and success. Little did I know that just a few years later, I would be in a very different place, one I never would have imagined for myself.

***

After that moment of realization, I tried to focus on what I knew for sure. I knew with certainty that I was living my life without joy. I knew I felt powerless and out of control. I wanted—needed—to do the things that most mattered to me so I could regain a sense of purpose.

Having spent seventeen years in safe corporate jobs, trying to balance a strict and antiquated definition of success with being a devoted mother, wife, daughter, friend, and member of multiple communities, I was finally ready to give myself permission to take a risk. I wanted to give myself the life I wanted to live.

Years earlier, a neighbor had told me about a master's program in spiritual psychology. When she mentioned it, I immediately put it into the growing category of things I'd like but would never get to do. After all, I'd never be able to fit it into my schedule, nor could I afford it. But after my epiphany, everything felt different. Suddenly it became an urgent need. I knew in every fiber of my being that this was exactly what I would do next.

So that same afternoon, as my son napped, I began poking around online. A couple of clicks later, I was staring at the website of the University of Santa Monica.

Spiritual psychology? I contemplated those words. I hadn't been looking for spirituality per se, though as I thought about it, I realized that I had always considered myself spiritual. I had always grappled with questions of purpose and meaning in the broadest context: why we're all here, and how to make the most of life. Though

I hadn't consciously been thinking about pursuing a psychology degree, I had been a psychology minor as an undergrad. I'd even studied organizational and consumer psychology in my MBA program. Those had in fact been my favorite courses—so much so that, upon graduation, I had momentarily wondered if I had gotten the wrong degree! I'd always been fascinated by how people think, feel, and make decisions. I had just forgotten that this side of me existed.

After my years in the corporate world, I found myself at a place where questions of self, identity, and purpose hit me with burning importance. The University of Santa Monica website stated that the program focused its curriculum around three key core questions:

1. Who am I?

2. What is my purpose?

3. How can I make a more meaningful contribution in my world?

These were precisely the questions I had been asking myself as far back as I could remember, and I couldn't wait another moment to find the answers. It seemed a forgone conclusion that this was my next step. That night I talked with my husband, Marc, about when I could quit my job, how we'd pay for the program, and whether I could really do this. A few weeks later, I was sitting at an informational session in a classroom filled with purple chairs, among faculty, alumni, and other prospective students. As I sat and listened to the presentation, I knew I was in the right place at the right time. When a former corporate lawyer on the alumni panel shared her experience in the program and the shift she had made to becoming a life coach, I gained confidence that it wasn't such a crazy idea. Even my parents might approve!

When the presentation concluded, I made a beeline to this lawyer-turned-coach so I could follow up with more questions. I picked up an application on my way out and walked on clouds back to the parking structure. It felt great to be excited about my future for the first time in years. It was a very different parking-structure moment.

The next morning, I went to work and gave notice. I started right away on my application and spent the next several months catching up on self-care and being a more present parent. I tended to personal and household projects I had long been neglecting. I finally began working with a physical therapist to heal my debilitating back pain, and I oversaw the list of repairs that needed to be done on our house. It felt incredibly strange and indulgent and a little bit wrong to not be working at a desk job. Nevertheless I felt light and buoyant—albeit somewhat filled with guilt.

When I received a letter of acceptance from the university, I was thrilled. I enrolled in the program that fall. My journey through it led me to a brand new definition of success. I began to recognize that there were things outside the realm of achievement that were equally—if not more—important to my inner peace, happiness, and well-being.

It was as if I had "seen the light." I found myself finally on a path to experiencing my life according to my values and priorities in all areas, beyond just my career. I realized how narrow my previous definition of success had been.

I began to take on a broader and more complete idea of success, one that considers the whole person in all aspects of life. I realized that career is just one part of the equation. I began thinking about life more holistically. It dawned on me that so many people I knew struggled with "work-life balance." They ran from work to home to their kids' soccer games, trying to squeeze it all in, often draining themselves in the process. Sleep? Health? Self-care? Those all got lost in the shuffle, but no one had time to think about it. People were running on empty.

The aspect of my program that illuminated this issue was the one I felt most self-conscious about: spirituality. Friends and former coworkers jokingly asked me if I was now burning incense and meditating in lotus position. Spirituality is not readily embraced by Western culture, and it's no wonder. With our Protestant roots, we try to maximize every day, working ourselves to the bone.

My new, holistic approach to success made me see life anew. It freed me from the constraints that had been making me miserable.

Armed with this new definition of success, I found my way to viewing myself as a successful person regardless of where I worked, what job I had, or how much I was recognized professionally. I began to see myself as successful at life. I saw that being true to oneself is what counts when measuring success.

I learned to recognize my needs, desires, and perceptions and honor them at each decision point. Doing so made it possible for me to act from a place of integrity, aligning my choices with what really mattered to me.

During this journey, I discovered that not everyone is hung up on his or her career. In my master's program, I encountered classmates from many walks of life. But, no matter their backgrounds, each one of them struggled with some area. For some, the career part was easy, but their relationships were filled with heartbreak and drama. For others, relationships were a breeze, but health problems were a source of tremendous stress. Still others were troubled by toxic family members, troubled marriages, drug or alcohol abuse, or general feelings of being lost or ill-equipped. Each person's definition of success differed depending on his or her unique circumstances. The more narrowly someone defined success, the more problems popped up. This is how I came to appreciate the need to recalibrate our understanding of success.

We each have our own set of expectations and dreams unique to our individual lives. Just as I had been wrong to believe that "arriving" in my career would bring fulfillment, others were flawed in thinking that plugging one hole in their lives would complete them.

The problem is, when we define success in a way that's too narrow, vague, and dependent on factors beyond our control, we get hyper focused on that one area and neglect other important parts of life. Then, when it feels that we aren't on track toward achieving our primary goal, we tend to judge ourselves as failures, regardless of the many other areas of life where we are thriving. We take those for granted.

As complex, multifaceted creatures, we are more than just one character trait. We are bound to feel discontented and unfulfilled if we measure our whole selves against one criterion.

Recognizing all this led me to conclude that a more expansive definition of success could benefit all of us, regardless of our individual struggles. For me, I discovered that while the pursuit of goals adds purpose and meaning to my life, and achievement is exhilarating in the short term, it's not everything. On its own, it doesn't guarantee a fulfilling life.

To be fulfilled as people, we need to take care of our whole selves and attempt to satisfy our needs across all areas of our lives. Maintaining a holistic balance helps us be the best versions of ourselves. The degree to which we can do that influences how we respond to whatever events and circumstances arise. When we can appreciate everything we are doing rather than focusing on what we're not doing, we can feel proud of who we are. We can be who we want to be in the world.

To me, this is authentic success. No job, salary, promotion, or accolades from a boss can provide lasting happiness or permanent success, just as no romantic partner or athletic accomplishment or dress size can guarantee fulfillment. Maintaining personal integrity by being true to ourselves means aligning our choices and actions with our deepest values and priorities.

If being true to one's self leads to deeper fulfillment, how do we stay true to ourselves? This book will share the fourteen most salient lessons, life skills, and tools to help you negotiate that process.

If you feel like your life isn't lining up with your hopes and expectations, you will get value out of this book. It doesn't matter what your personal struggles are. Whether your goals and ideas of success revolve around career, relationships, parenting, health, finances, or self-worth, the lessons in this book are applicable.

What sets this book apart from others that discuss balance and fulfillment is its emphasis on practicality and day-to-day life. It is divided into concrete, manageable lessons explained in a way that's meant to make them easy for you to implement. At the back of this book, you will find exercises that correspond to each lesson and are designed to assist you in applying the concepts to your own life. They are there for you as a resource. Whether you plan to do an exercise right away after you've read a lesson, or after you finish the entire book, I recommend taking a look at each one before continuing to the next lesson.

If you take the time to really absorb the lessons and commit to doing the exercises, you will be well on your way to working through your recurring issues. You will gain clarity to make better decisions, let go of unrealistic expectations, be kinder, gentler, and more forgiving toward yourself, and create a path of ease and grace as you work toward your goals.

WHY DO WE NEED TO REDEFINE SUCCESS, ANYWAY?

What a Limited Definition of Success Looks Like

When we define success narrowly, investing too much energy in one area, we fail to thrive. Our spirits suffer. In my case, for example, when I defined personal success solely through the lens of my career, I was exhausted, insecure, and consumed by anxiety. I was driven by the desire to get to the bottom of my never-ending to-do list.

Here is what a typical day looked like for me. In the mornings, I leaped out of bed and rushed to exercise before my son woke up. Afterward, I set his breakfast up on a bench in our bathroom so I could supervise him while I showered. Then I raced to get us both dressed and out the door to his daycare. I typically arrived late to work, thanking God that my company wasn't a stickler about that. At the office, I ran from one meeting to the next all day long. The thinking, planning, research, analysis, writing, and communicating with my team—what I thought of as my *actual* work—had to be squeezed into the cracks of my workday. Ten minutes here, ten minutes there, half an hour during lunchtime if I was lucky. This meant I would only just be getting started on the bulk of my responsibilities at the end of the day, and I would stay late in a desperate attempt to bring at least one task to a close—while also feeling pressure to wrap up so I could spend time with my family.

I worked for a "direct response" fitness company that sold its products via infomercials. The beauty of our sales model was that we had instant data we could use to optimize sales. The downside was that we were constantly chasing those improvements. Any delay could result in missed sales opportunities. Each time we changed our offers, we had to involve large teams of people across different parts of the organization.

At first it was exciting work. But over time the frantic pace wore me down. The job became unsatisfying and frustrating. I was constantly afraid of getting fired. My family needed my income. I worried what would happen if I lost this job I hated so much. I felt like I was always spinning my wheels, but in a race to nowhere.

By the time I got home, it was 7:00 p.m. I'd be exhausted, my nervous system fried. And yet there was so much to be done at home. Naturally, I couldn't wait to spend time with my son: playing, reading, and putting him to bed. But at the tail end of the night, as the big hand made its way around the clock, it also seemed to wind up my insides. I would panic, knowing I still faced all of the minutiae of daily life: meal planning, laundry, cleaning, scheduling, cooking. Marc traveled frequently for work, leaving me on my own to navigate the myriad challenges of having a young child.

I felt like I had no control over my life. I perceived myself to be a step behind across the board, which was unnerving for me, as someone who took pride in being one step ahead. I lived with an ever-present feeling that if anyone were to give me just one more thing to do, I might fall apart.

Much of this will sound familiar in our overworked culture. Being overextended and stressed out is the norm these days. More families than ever consist of two working parents, both facing considerable pressure in their jobs. Bombarded with a constant stream of articles and studies, we feel a second dose of pressure at home. How are we to feel safe when we're constantly hearing about new dangers and threats? The sun causes harm and so does the sunscreen! Overuse of antibiotics is breeding drug-resistant superbugs! Advice comes at us from all angles about how we can be better parents. Let them cry, don't let them cry. Keep them safe in the big bad world, but don't be a helicopter parent. The result is that we're constantly playing whack-a-mole. We aren't thinking about how we **want** to live our lives. We're too busy scrambling from day to day, hoping to get everything done and not make any catastrophic mistakes along the way.

How can you tell if your definition of success is too limited? Below are some of the common dynamics we experience when we live with a constricted definition of success.

1. Constant Guilt

When our definition of success is limited, we don't give ourselves permission to relax—nor do we give ourselves credit for all that we do. In my own life, I experienced guilt coming at me from all directions. At work, I felt guilty for not being home with my son as much as I felt I should, while at the same time, I felt guilty for not being able to focus singularly on my job the way I'd always done in the past, before becoming a mother. I looked at my "first-world problems" and judged myself as ungrateful for my privilege. A narrow definition of success doesn't provide us with full, healthy options for how life can look.

2. Comparing Ourselves to Others

These days, social media culture invites us to compare ourselves to others constantly. Typically this points us to the conclusion that we don't measure up.

My quest for success fueled this habit in me. I compared myself not just to my colleagues but also to other moms—those who worked and those who didn't. My thoughts and actions were dominated by unrealistic expectations, both those I generated for myself and those I **perceived** others to have of me. Never mind if they were real or imagined, or if they even reflected what actually mattered to me; I fixated on trying to meet them.

I took it as fact that I lacked competence, and then attributed it to personal deficiency. Through this distorted lens, I looked at other working mothers and regarded them as having figured it all out. I marveled at them and further diminished myself.

As a consummate learner, I wondered, practically speaking, how those supermoms did it. My inner optimist believed there might actually be some trick, a simple hack to manage it all. I was driven to keep searching and questioning in hopes that someone might have the formula and be willing to share it with me. This desire to crack the secret code became yet another item on my plate. It also kept me from recognizing and appreciating myself for the incredible job I was already doing—and from having compassion for myself as I faced **real-world**, grown-up human difficulties.

3. Perfectionism

Comparing ourselves to others often goes hand in hand with perfectionism. We don't give ourselves permission to experiment and make mistakes. We often find ourselves preoccupied by endless opportunities for improvement. Perfectionism is like a permanent itch demanding to be scratched, depriving us of the feeling of pride in a job well done.

In my life, perfectionism was a double-edged sword, with self-doubt on one side and overconfidence on the other. I held myself to an unnecessarily high standard. I believed that I could accomplish anything if I simply worked hard enough. Thus, I could never allow myself to let something slip through the cracks or let anyone down in any way, ever. I couldn't allow myself to be *human*.

I was terrified of making a mistake. I didn't want to be responsible for the repercussions of an oversight, and the mere possibility of the shame I'd feel as a result was like an ever-present threat lurking around the corner. My desire for perfection paralyzed me. My education, skills, and work experience did nothing to help. This is how perfectionism looks and feels. It creates shaky ground where we don't trust ourselves. We overthink, overanalyze, and second-guess every decision. Nothing is ever good enough, and we take everything personally, as if it reflects who we are as human beings and determines our worth and value in the world.

4. Control

People who are high achievers or generally overly taxed take refuge in the idea of control. My expectation that I could accomplish everything through proper planning and organization drove me to attempt to optimize all aspects of my life. As I strove for 100 percent efficiency, it felt like there was no slack in the operation of my life. I tried to predict life's every move and line everything up, but unexpected circumstances always arose, infuriating me. I would blame myself for not waking up earlier, getting ready faster, knowing more, or being a little more willing to let go of the nonessentials. I felt tormented living that way. There was no room for spontaneity, and my life felt oppressive.

When we attempt to achieve our goals by working harder and trying to control everything even more tightly, we end up feeling even more **out of control**, not to mention fragmented and overwhelmed.

5. Lack of Self-Care and Joy

When our view of success is limited, we don't take sufficient care of ourselves or allow joy into our lives. I didn't even bother trying to squeeze time for myself into my schedule. I was always taking care of every**thing** and everyone **else**. I was last in line. Addressing my own needs simply wasn't a priority.

Perhaps my favorite part of my workday was going to the bathroom. It must sound so odd, but that was the only time that was just for me. The bathroom was the only place I could zone out and not get interrupted—unless I was at home, in which case I was guaranteed to have Cooper as an audience. At work, I'd lock the stall door and sit and breathe. I've since learned how common this is among moms. The bathroom—of all places—should not be the sole place in one's life for self-care. Yet too many of us, if we didn't have to stop to go to the bathroom, wouldn't stop at all.

As I learned to recalibrate my view of success, I came up with something that I called "FIGL." This stood for "Fuck It, I'm Going to Lunch." Tongue in cheek, it represented my meager attempt to defend my sanity and claim some time for myself—outside of the bathroom. There was a conscious attitude of rebellion to it. I'd wolf down my previous night's leftovers at my desk and then take thirty minutes to read outside on the balcony or walk to a nearby park. It gave me time to breathe fresh air and feel the sunshine on my skin. I did this once or twice a week and learned that the world didn't end. This small guilty pleasure recharged me and made the day a smidgen more bearable. Self-care is crucial to our well-being, and yet it so often gets compromised.

6. Not Being Fully Available to Others

When we don't take time for ourselves to refuel, it's difficult to be loving, present, and fully engaged with others. When we're depleted physically, emotionally, and spiritually, our energy gets drained. My family got more attention from me than I gave myself, but they still paid a price. In being perpetually exhausted and preoccupied by my worries and fears, I wasn't bringing home the prime cuts of myself. My family was getting the picked-over remains. Marc had to live with an insecure, unhappy wife who was constantly fretting about one or another stalled project at work. Cooper had a loving but anxious mother.

Moments that could have been sweet and joyful were instead stressful for everyone. Out on an errand, for example, if Cooper wanted to stop and touch everything (as toddlers often do), I would become a wreck. I was so panicked about falling behind schedule that I rushed him along. The pressure I felt was palpable and ever present.

Like any child, Cooper deserved to follow his curiosity—to stop to pick up a snail, examine a flower, jump in a puddle, explore the sensation of a brick wall. These are vital parts of childhood. I also deserved to be present and relaxed during those small, magical—and fleeting—moments. I deserved to have the opportunity to see the world through his eyes and experience the awe and wonder of life alongside him. He was doing exactly what a toddler should do, but my anxiety led me to respond as if he were misbehaving. I was asking him to adapt to my needs rather than honoring his, when it should have been the other way around. My impossible expectations weren't fair to either of us.

What Changes When We Adopt a More Expansive Definition of Success

What happens when we broaden our criteria for success and fulfillment? The first thing is that we expand the scope of what we consider our identity.

The decision to expand our view of success brings into play our core values as human beings. We hear the word "success" and perhaps think of material goods or observable measures. But really, so much of what matters most to us can't be easily measured. Who we are, how we go about the world–these are perhaps invisible, but they are of infinite importance.

In my case, I learned that my career is not who *I am*. My job is a place I put my time. It's a way to generate income. It may help me grow by challenging me and offering a context for me to engage my creativity and intellect. I may derive fulfillment from it, and my job may even enhance my social life. Certainly, there will be ups and downs. But it's *not* who I am. *I* am so much more. My job is just something that I *do*. We never stop being who we are, no matter what job we're doing. You can think about it by asking yourself: "Without my job, do I still exist?" Of course you do!

Success goes beyond our titles, beyond excelling and receiving recognition in our careers. Success comes from knowing what matters to us across all catego-ries of our lives and being true to ourselves by living accordingly. It also comes from learning how to both cope more productively with inevitable stress and culti-vate the inherent joys in life. As Anthony Robbins says, "Live life fully while you're here. Experience everything. Take care of yourself and your friends. Have fun, be crazy, be weird. Go out and screw up! You're going to anyway, so you might as well enjoy the process. Take the opportunity to learn from your mistakes: find the cause of your problem and eliminate it. Don't try to be perfect; just be an excellent example of being human." When we release beliefs and thought patterns that no longer serve us, we discover that we are already successful.

There are healthy mindsets and ways of approaching life that can help us feel centered, balanced, and whole. These techniques—which I've refined into the fourteen lessons that form this book—can help you become your best self. When you combine these skills and techniques with your expanded definition of success, you will notice yourself engaging with the world in ways you may not have previously imagined. Your new way of being will become the starting point for success that is both profound and authentic to you.

It's a Process!

The benefits of expanding our definition of success seem clear. But there's one point I can't emphasize enough: this isn't a set-it-and-forget-it situation. An expanded mindset is a great starting point, but if you want to consistently show up as your best self, you have to apply the skills on an ongoing basis. Like exercise, it's a daily and lifelong commitment. A practice. So be gentle, patient, and forgiving with yourself.

In my own life, after graduating with my master's from the spirituality program, I felt liberated. I was finally able to experience inner peace and exist in a calm state, even when faced with obstacles. It was amazing! And it even lasted...for a good year or two.

What changed? I'd had a second child by then, an incredible baby girl. I was back to working—on this book and as a life coach. My life began to creep back into familiar territory, with all my old feelings of stress, anxiety, guilt, and loss of control.

I learned two valuable lessons from this. Number one, my career wasn't the source of my issues. It just pushed my personal patterns to the surface. And number two, though the insights I'd gained were useful, they didn't guarantee eternal happiness. While I had figured out how to stay in touch with my top priorities, take ownership of my choices, and assume responsibility for my attitude, it became evident that striving to be my best was an ongoing process and journey. We don't learn these lessons once. We constantly relearn them, acquiring a deeper level of mastery each time.

I had climbed a rung or two on my own ladder of growth and had reached a beautiful lookout point. While this was indeed a giant step forward in my life journey, I couldn't stay there forever. It was one iteration of my growth and my ability to accept life as it is. But life marches forward, and, as I discovered yet again, our journeys include many traffic jams and detours, long stretches of hinterland, and—when we're lucky—brief, light, and joy-filled respites from it all.

The opportunity for more growth is good news. No matter where we are in our lives, we know that there are challenges ahead. There is always room to develop ourselves further. Life is a series of invitations to grow in wisdom. We can continually deepen our understanding of who we are, why we're here, and how we can make our greatest contribution.

This fourteen core lessons of this book aren't meant to be simply read and conquered. They are guideposts to help you on your ongoing journey. One way to think of them is akin to an automotive shop's multi-point inspection checklist: When feeling emotionally off balance or in need of some "repair work," you can refer back to them as a way of discovering where your system is off. And you can revisit the related exercises to help restore yourself.

THE OBSTACLES BETWEEN YOU AND THE LIFE YOU WANT

Before diving into the lessons of this book, let's examine some of the obstacles that may be blocking you from the life you want to lead. We all have mental blocks that can prevent us from moving forward toward our goals. Unless we dismantle and address those hurdles, real progress can be difficult to achieve.

As we go through life, we accumulate a set of beliefs informed by our experiences. Sometimes these beliefs cause blind spots. They get so ingrained that we don't notice when they no longer apply or when they're not serving us well. That's what happened to me, and it happens to many of us.

For example, I felt compelled to stick with my career because of limiting and unsupportive subconscious beliefs that I justified as "sound judgment." Someone with **sound judgment** wouldn't quit her job. Someone with **sound judgment** wouldn't go back for a second master's degree—especially one in spirituality. This was how my inner critic kept me fettered: through judgments that seemed like they were in my best interest.

This is an example of how psychological obstacles manifest. They are embedded in our thought patterns. They spring up without our even realizing it—without feeling like blocks at all. Three common blocks people experience are:

1. Misconceptions about success

2. Fear of failure

3. Beliefs about money

Misconceptions About Success

Oftentimes the roots of our obstacles go back to childhood. In my case, growing up, my entire frame of reference was oriented around ensuring "success" in life. The problem was, the meaning of success was never explicitly discussed. It wasn't as though my parents ever sat me down to tell me that when I grew up I'd need to fall within a certain income bracket or that I needed to pursue status. But the people I was surrounded by seemed to possess impressive status and wealth—and from their conversations, it was apparent that they felt this put them in a class above the rest. There's no doubt that my parents would have been delighted to see me attain great wealth and status—I mean, whose wouldn't? But I know that, most of all, they wanted me to become a happy, well-adjusted, and well-rounded individual.

One message that was very clear was the value they placed on hard work and achievement. Working hard—moreover, setting personal needs aside in order to put work first—was an important determinant of an individual's worth and value. Somehow, these ideas of personal achievement, money, and status got wrapped up together in a single package. And it's the ideas we absorb **unconsciously** that can be the most difficult to unpack.

I got in the habit of studying hard, believing that if I earned good grades in high school, I'd get into a good college, and—*voila!*—I'd be set for life. I would become successful. Since I didn't know what success meant, status and money became its proxies. They would confirm, or deny, my worth as a person.

There are two big problems with having such a narrow view of success. First, status and money aren't natural motivators for everyone. Second, if we don't find our way to attaining that limited definition of success, the natural conclusion is that we are failures.

When we define our level of success based on external yardsticks, we miss discovering our internal measures of fulfillment. In adulthood, when we have more choices about what to do with our lives, we need to know what we're chasing. When it's no longer about earning the grades, or about something as concrete as getting into college or landing a particular job, trying to determine how well we're doing can become messy.

When we don't know what success looks like for us, but we keep pushing ourselves as if we did, we put ourselves on a path to burnout and discontent. Life doesn't operate on a semester system, with its comforting series of finite beginnings and ends, and with breaks in between.

We need to know our own personal definitions of success and not just accept by default the ones handed down to us by others. We need to know the purpose behind our efforts so we can put our time and energy into areas that matter to *us*. Otherwise, we risk pushing ourselves for the sake of pushing. While striving for its own sake can sometimes feel fulfilling, if it's not something we truly enjoy and it doesn't lead to what matters to us on a deeper level, we'll eventually run out of steam.

Because I never thought to question my path, I tried to stay on it—to keep finding ways of achieving. I looked for steady, full-time jobs and continued to press play on the old recording:

WORK HARD

GET "GOOD GRADES" (this time in the form of recognition, promotions, a nice salary, etc.)

BE HAPPY AND "SUCCESSFUL"

I gave it a go in many different sectors—nonprofit, government, and for-profit sales and marketing. But none of the jobs I tried brought me happiness or fulfillment, because I didn't know what I was looking for beyond "good grades," which had taken on a new form as workplace validation: recognition, promotions, and raises.

Fear of Failure

Most of us fear failure, though that fear manifests in different ways. We might fear letting down family or embarrassing ourselves in public. Some people have anxiety dreams about getting fired, while others may avoid pursuing a dream because life feels "safer" that way.

In my case, growing up, "stick-to-it-iveness" was a key value prized by my family. Quitting, on the other hand, was almost a mortal sin. We Wolks simply were not "quitters."

Much like "success" and "hard work," the nuances of "quitting" were never explored, and as a result, without even realizing it, I adopted an overly broad interpretation of what constituted quitting. Unconsciously, I came to regard it as unacceptable under **any** circumstances. Anything that resembled throwing in the towel just wasn't an option. Because I had never seen a precedent for quitting without having a "better" opportunity lined up, my perspective was skewed. It didn't occur to me that we sometimes have to walk away from what we know isn't working, even if we don't have something better lined up.

When we walk away from the things (or people) that drain us, we free ourselves. We create space for something new and room for improved versions of ourselves. Anthony Robbins has reflected, "I've come to believe that all my past failure and frustration were actually laying the foundation for the understandings that have created the new level of living I now enjoy."

Because the prospect of leaving my career altogether seemed so unfathomable from a rational perspective, the only way I could act upon it was to take a leap of faith. I had to dive into the unknown and trust that I would land on my feet. Sometimes we have to take the risk to reap the reward.

Beliefs About Money

Everyone has different beliefs about money, and these can be deeply ingrained in us. We don't necessarily give them conscious thought, but they surface in our choices, especially during times of stress. Our feelings about and approaches toward money are tied intrinsically to how we were raised. No wonder money is one of the top three issues couples fight over; it's a thorny and fraught subject. Whether we grew up in challenging environments or relatively privileged circumstances, whether money was abundant or scarce, our attitudes toward it can hold us back.

In my case, I had to release beliefs I had assimilated from my upbringing regarding fiscal responsibility and self-sufficiency. Unlike the idea of success, these ideals were instilled in me explicitly through my parents' words and actions. I took their message deeply to heart, and it developed into a core personal value. I learned to believe, in fact, that people could be divided between good and bad based on fiscal responsibility and self-sufficiency. In other words, on some level, I tied money to morality.

To be fiscally responsible and self-sufficient required considering only safe and secure career options, meaning jobs that provided health insurance and a steady paycheck. That ruled out a lot of options—perhaps the very options that actually could have given me an authentic sense of purpose and meaning.

A feeling of responsibility drove my choices. In the early of years of my marriage, I was the primary breadwinner while my husband pursued entrepreneurship. We relied heavily on my income to keep us afloat. When the Great Recession hit and the economy collapsed, we panicked. My husband was working on a business he had founded. Its survival would be determined by his ability to attract funding. Before the recession, we'd believed he had a reasonable chance of getting that funding. Now it seemed clear that he wouldn't. Meanwhile, I became pregnant.

As a new father, he decided to take a steady job and found one with a reputable company. But that didn't give me the comfort I needed. I still told myself I couldn't possibly leave my job. That would have conflicted too head-on with my values. In essence, I had grown to view almost *everything* in life through a financial lens and made decisions accordingly.

Even if it hadn't been for the recession, I'd had a lifelong, irrational fear of running out of money. This fear was likely handed down unconsciously through the generations. Our associations with money can have deep cultural roots and familial baggage. My mother, for example, was a fervent coupon-clipper, as was her mother before her. Growing up, the need to comparison shop was drilled into me. As an adult, I could never hand over my credit card until I had exhausted enough options to feel confident that I had found the best deal. Frugality became my way of staving off potential poverty.

My career soothed this fear. It addressed my fiscal requirements, plus it gave me structure: a place to go each day, a schedule, and a social life. I worked alongside intelligent peers and enjoyed the collaboration, the camaraderie, and the friendships. Each day, I felt productive as part of a system and derived purpose and pleasure as a key contributor in creating something of tangible value. I got a behind-the-scenes peek at how products were conceived, developed, brought to market, and sold. I was learning—and building my resumé. I told myself it was enough.

I didn't understand how much my deep anxieties regarding money weighed on me—and drained me. I wasn't giving myself permission to be fully myself. To navigate into a new trajectory in my life, I needed to shake off my financial lens. Being self-sufficient and fiscally responsible can be pragmatic. But it can also foster a scarcity mindset that is narrow and restrictive.

It can blind us to more expansive perspectives and possibilities.

Our hang-ups about money can create a whole set of false beliefs that don't serve us. We use money to rationalize situations where we feel trapped. We tell ourselves we have no options, for example: that we can't possibly switch careers or go back to school or move to another place. We put ourselves in prisons and tell ourselves money is the reason. In my case, I could have won the lottery and still found reasons to be miserable. The problem was in my mindset, not in my bank account.

Money can often be an excuse for avoiding deeper problems. For me, it was an excuse not to take responsibility for creating a life that would be a better fit for me and my family. The truth was, beneath my rational argument about financial sensibleness, I was *afraid*. Afraid of the unknown. Afraid of giving up my status as a stressed-out victim. And afraid of taking responsibility for my own happiness. I knew that if I pointed to money as the culprit, I could hide behind it. Without money as my shield, I'd have no one to blame but myself.

I had no idea at the time that I would one day come to recognize this leap of faith as my first step toward having faith in *myself*. I didn't know that I was about to embark on a full-scale spiritual journey.

To truly confront the obstacles that are holding us back, whether they concern success, failure, or money, requires us to dig deep. It involves an existential inquiry into who we really are and who we wish to be. No wonder we tell ourselves we can't possibly change our lives. To do so risks throwing our assumed beliefs into crisis! That's why the first lesson of this book involves spirituality. My own journey down that path became the foundation for all of the lessons in this book. Beginning here offers tremendous potential for all of us.

LESSONS

LESSON 1
SPIRIT

If you'd asked me years ago, I would have laughed at the idea of spirituality becoming an integral part of my life. Like many driven, type-A, corporate sorts, I was focused almost exclusively on achievement. I read articles on topics like productivity, time management, and being a woman in the workplace. The prospect of one day enthusiastically embracing Spirit would have struck me as crazy.

And yet, as far back as I could remember, I had questioned the meaning of life. I desperately wanted to find my purpose and feel that I was making a positive difference in the world.

Over the course of my journey, I began to more actively consider the spiritual context as I faced everyday ups and downs. As this way of looking at life made its way to the forefront of my mind, my understanding of the role of Spirit began to crystallize intellectually. Before long, I began to process and interpret everything that was happening through the lens of spirituality and factor its lessons into my thoughts, attitude, and actions. Over time, I grew to recognize Spirit as a source I could draw upon to lessen stress, self-doubt, and the desire to please. Worry and indecision faded away. I began to experience more ease and grace in my daily life. I took on a much more hopeful outlook—based not on unrealistic expectations or wishful thinking but rather on genuine *trust* in the Universe.

Painting the Picture

Before I get into detail about how Spirit—and, more specifically, partnering with it—can enhance your life, I want to paint you a picture. Close your eyes. Imagine elevating your perspective: zooming out beyond your home, block, city, state. Keep zooming out until you're above your country, above the planet. Then go out into the stars. You're now above our solar system, floating beyond to other solar systems, where space is infinite and time is irrelevant. The idea that human concerns are minuscule isn't meant to make us feel irrelevant but rather to liberate us.

This picture is the essence of what Spirit entails. We could call it God, but we don't need to. Some people call it Source, Creation, or Divine Intelligence. Throughout this book, you may see me refer to Spirit interchangeably by other names, most frequently, the Universe, Life, Authentic Self. Just as there are many names for it, there are also countless everyday qualities associated with it: wisdom, beauty, enthusiasm, and inner peace, to name a few of my personal favorites. You'll find many more sprinkled throughout this book, because all of the qualities we experience as uplifting and inspiring are synonymous with Spirit.

Regardless of the name, you can think of Spirit as an energy field, a higher power or force, or an organizing intelligence behind all of life. In this way, Spirit is invisible. Yet it is also fully perceptible, considering that it manifests itself in the physical universe: every life form (and even death), every thought, feeling, action, event, circumstance, you name it. It's *everything*.

Spirit is infinite and connects the souls of all living creatures and forms across time and space. It's you, it's me, it's the mountains, the ocean, a flower, a snowflake. It's music, ideas, creations, inventions, our hopes, our dreams, and even our tragedies. It's our relationship to all of those things as well as how we interact with each one. We are all equally a part of it. In fact, it is the sum of everything around us. It's impossible for anyone or anything to be separate from it. As the poet Rumi said, "You are not a drop in the ocean. You are the entire ocean in a drop."

You don't have to be a "spiritual person" to understand the power of the Universe. You need only look at the material world in front of you to recognize our own relative powerlessness and, in many ways, insignificance.

This isn't meant to belittle our everyday concerns but rather to remind us of our transience.

As much as we might want to believe in our own agency, our capacity to influence what goes on around us is limited. From this vantage point, how could we deny that we ultimately work in partnership with all of Life? To think that we are acting alone thus appears ridiculous. It becomes obvious that we don't control much at all. Relative to the infinite nature of time and space, how much do our tiny goals, flaws, issues, and upsets even matter?

It's really quite absurd to think of all the ways in which we try to control Life. We give ourselves such a hard time unnecessarily when we judge ourselves and others. We focus on our shortcomings and beat ourselves up, compare ourselves, fret over our decisions, and sometimes hurt others to get what we want. When we look at our lives from an elevated perspective, our pettiness can seem…well, petty. Anger and judgment fade. Acceptance and kindness become more intuitive. Looking at life from a higher altitude reveals that we do have a choice when it comes to our thoughts and behaviors. Why not just make the choice to love rather than to hate, fear, and judge? After all, we feel better when we choose love.

The human ego is reluctant to cede control. It tells us that we are smart, special, and powerful. It lures us into thinking we have control. It does not want to acknowledge that some of our choices may be inconsequential. But if we sit with this idea, if we let go of the ego, many of our petty judgments, our anxieties, and our anger simply fall away in the grand scheme of things. This can be liberating—a relief.

If we view ourselves as tiny pieces of a greater whole, we see that we are exactly as we should be. We are absolutely perfect as we are. In fact, this is just one of many contradictory truths within the spiritual context. This is also why, when we do get angry, confused, or filled with self-doubt, it makes so much sense to set aside a few moments to reflect on the big picture. When we are most stressed out, most squeezed for time, most convinced that we can't take a few deep breaths or meditate, this is precisely when we most need to do so. This is one of the ways we can nurture our connection with Spirit and help take a bit of pressure off ourselves.

Spirit and Growth

Spirituality shows us that our purpose through our life's journey is **to learn from our experiences so we can grow and evolve into more loving and compassionate beings**. If we consider the perspective that we are not mere mortals, but rather eternal souls temporarily inhabiting physical human bodies in order to have the *opportunity* to go through certain struggles, then we see those struggles for what they really are: growth opportunities. Any challenges are part of our own personal curriculum in "life school," as my professors often call it. And as we progress through this curriculum, we may use our challenges to resolve or "heal" recurring issues, move beyond patterns that don't serve us, and learn how (and when) to nurture ourselves such that we can become the best, most loving versions of ourselves.

Viewing our struggles in this way helps us see that they are not punishments, nor do they mean anything in and of themselves. Instead, we may view them as advanced coursework in our learning journeys. The more evolved we are in our understanding, the more we may even be able to regard them as a gift or blessing. If we approach them consciously and manage to resolve an issue, we can graduate to the next level in our soul's evolution.

You will recognize your own evolution as you become wiser and more connected with your authentic self, which is always confident, loving, and compassionate. If this is why we are here on earth, then all that really matters is where we are in a particular moment. Every struggle is one point in time relative to your own soul's journey.

The second part of our purpose has to do with our relationship to the Whole. Since we are each bumping around with all the other souls on our planet, how we show up and the kind of energy we put forth makes a difference. Our thoughts, deeds, and actions have tangible ripple effects. Spiritually speaking, our own personal evolution is important not only for ourselves but also in terms of how we contribute to the world around us. As we heal our wounds and learn to relate to ourselves with more kindness, gentleness, and acceptance, we get closer to our own essential loving nature. It becomes easier to be a source of love and compassion to others as well.

Assumptions About Spirit

There are some important assumptions that go along with having a genuine belief in Spirit:

1. Since the purpose of our journey is to learn and grow, the Universe's job is not to make our lives easy, but rather to put experiences in our path to help us evolve. While it may push us right up to our limit, it won't give us anything we can't handle.

2. We are not alone or without resources and support. The Universe is limitless and will provide what we need. Furthermore, we are allowed to ask for what we need. This idea should provide us comfort during particularly challenging times.

3. Fellow humans are an emanation and expression of Spirit. We are interconnected and meant to rely on one another. If each of us is part of the Whole, a droplet of the same ocean, then it follows that each of us has the internal resources we need to resolve any issue, problem, or challenge.

These notions should give us confidence that even when we suffer, we can get through whatever we're given and that our essential Selves will be okay. Because there is an intelligence to the Universe, our whole experience will be for our highest good. If we can find our way to believing all of this, we can **trust** life. This trust enables us to see that whatever the Universe is putting us through is meant **for** us. The Universe is not **against** us. It's a gift and a blessing for our highest good across time.

These foundations help us approach life with generosity and abundance. Everything is available to us and **accessible**, as long as we are able to establish our connection to Source. In secular terms, what I mean by "connection to Source" is taking a moment to remember that we are operating within and in partnership with a larger picture. Though this connection waxes and wanes over time, it is always at our disposal to provide assistance when we need it. It will never hold a grudge against us for the times we haven't nurtured our connection to it. We just need to call upon it.

A spiritual orientation to life isn't reserved for the shamans, yogis, and mediums among us. It's possible for everyone. You do not need to convert into a "spiritual person" or make any radical changes to who you are or how you see yourself. In fact, I'm willing to bet that you might already have intuition about spirituality that isn't far off from what I've described.

Let's explore a few examples of how you might already be spiritually attuned, possibly without even knowing it. If you love being out in nature, surfing, cooking, listening to music, dancing, painting, or even just laughing with friends—and you find that these activities recharge you—then you know what it's like to connect with Spirit. This feeling of being refueled and enlivened is an experience of Spirit. To be in the flow of these activities, to be immersed in the moment—this is a manifestation of spirituality. When we let go of ourselves, we enter the spiritual world. One of the most powerful manifestations of spirituality is the experience of loving others. Whether the object of our love is a parent, child, spouse, or four-legged friend, the feeling that wells up in our hearts and can bring tears of joy to our eyes is the essence of spirituality. And anytime we engage in these activities or think of these loved ones, we are reinforcing our connection to Spirit.

Applying Spirituality: Presence

How can we use this theoretical understanding of Spirit to improve our lives on a practical level? (As a pragmatist, I know that's the part *I* care about.) How do we take these broad concepts and apply them so we can reap their benefits?

We can reestablish our awareness of Spirit through presence. Presence is the access point to Spirit. This means focusing on the *moment*, which is a tool available to everyone—though it is not always easy to achieve.

We've all had the experience of being overwhelmed or panicked. I remember one day when I volunteered for Cooper's class field trip. He was excited; I wanted the day to go perfectly. As we pulled up to the school, however, I saw with a sinking feeling that parking was pure chaos. It turned out there were other events scheduled that day. As I circled the block, I watched the clock tick and my heart began to race. To my chagrin, we were now running late. Cooper began to panic, and before I knew it, I had broken into a sweat.

I soon realized that there was nothing I could do. Anxiety wasn't going to miraculously manifest a previously unnoticed parking spot. My best option was to surrender to the moment. So I did just that. As soon as I was able to bring my awareness back to the present, I was freed from my panic. My presence enabled me to see with clarity that, while the situation wasn't ideal, *we* were fine. No one was sick, nor was there any danger. We would handle being a bit late. This restored my inner feeling of peace, which in turn allowed me to reassure Cooper that everything was okay.

When we focus our attention on the now, we are able to elevate our thinking. This is true whether it's a momentarily stressful situation, like being late for an event, or a more serious set of circumstances. In particularly difficult situations, cultivating presence can anchor us. We may never have complete certainty or clarity on why bad things happen, but if we can find a way to trust in Spirit's wisdom, we may find the seemingly arbitrary nature of life less threatening. A spiritual mindset may not change our circumstances, but it can calm us. When we are able to accept the moment as it is, we are more likely to experience inner peace and hope.

Being present allows us to take in our body's sensations, which are invaluable feedback mechanisms. When we stop and notice our racing pulse, it slows. Trying to ignore our symptoms causes them to worsen. As psychologist Carl Jung once said, "What you resist…persists." From a present state, we can interpret our body's feedback. We can then respond in a way that aligns with what we desire and how we want to be in the world. Ultimately, this enables us to feel good about our actions.

A friend of mine recently confided in me that she was debating whether or not to text a guy she was dating. Five days earlier, they had inadvertently stepped into a serious conversation about what they were looking for in a romantic relationship, and they hadn't spoken since. Naturally, she couldn't help wondering what that meant. Had something gone awry, or was he just busy?

As she shared this situation with me, I asked her to pause, take a deep breath, and ask where the impulse to reach out to him was coming from. Closing her eyes and considering this, she realized that the urge was not coming from the desire to talk to him, but rather from an insecure place of wanting validation that he found her desirable. That was not the kind of motivation she wanted to act upon.

It wasn't a terribly comforting realization, but she understood that she would benefit from doing some internal work to validate herself. She saw that she didn't want to turn to a man just to be found desirable.

While she didn't come out of our conversation with all the answers, she saw her immediate next step, which was to refrain from saying anything at all. She knew she didn't want to initiate communication for reasons that didn't match her ideals. As long as she committed to staying present, she would have clarity about what to do next. She would have integrity.

When we're upset or worried, bringing our awareness to the present moment illuminates what's truly bothering us. It helps us differentiate between a real problem and a story we're telling ourselves—one that likely isn't relevant to the moment at hand. In the example above, my friend wasn't really concerned about that relationship. She felt insecure about her worth. Without realizing it, she'd been telling herself that she wasn't worthy. Texting with him wasn't going to resolve her real issue. The more we practice presence, the more skilled we become at consciously tuning in to our feelings. We become more aware of what's truly going on.

Presence enables us to see what we need to act on *now*. When we root ourselves in the present moment, we catch ourselves playing out scenarios and hypotheticals that haven't actually transpired. This awareness can help remove a lot of the pressure we put on ourselves.

Until we catch up in time to the future, we are assuredly better off *not* making any decisions or taking premature action. We will acquire more information in the meantime that helps us make more informed decisions when the time comes.

As we learn to become more present, life feels richer and fuller. Once I stopped listening to the white noise of worries and anxieties, I discovered that most of the things that brought me joy were very simple and accessible. I noticed the depth of beauty in small joys: doing Legos with my son, going to the library with my daughter, unexpectedly bumping into a friend, hearing birds chirping, feeling warm sun or a cool breeze on my skin, dancing with my children.

A virtuous cycle ensues. The more mindful we are of simple pleasures, the more they seem to show up. The more we witness joy, the more gratitude we feel for its abundance. It's as though we turn up the volume on the positive by being mindful. We can then adjust life to proactively invite in even more joy. Once we know how much we love to dance, we can set aside time for it. If we know we enjoy being kind, we are less aggravated by a small interruption in the day, recognizing it as an opportunity to practice kindness. These small shifts can have a profound effect on us.

When we're present, we know what we need to do. For example, rather than getting mad, blaming someone (oftentimes yourself), or feeling as though life is unfair, you can ask yourself questions such as "Where does this experience fit into the bigger, longer-term picture of my life?" or "What can I learn from this situation?" When you ask such questions, you allow the crisis to become the opportunity.

This idea is so contrary to how many of us operate. It can be difficult to give up control, particularly when we're used to applying our will, smarts, and discipline to achieve our goals. During moments of crisis, we want to find solutions to will our way out of the problem, instead of accepting that the Universe may have a lesson for us. When we ask Spirit to provide us the assistance we desire and draw our awareness to the present moment, we become more efficient and effective across all areas of our lives.

Think about it: Like all of us, you've probably experienced that moment of trying to find a way through a project or a solution to a work problem, only to sit at your desk and feel stumped. You stare at your computer screen or look at the same document a hundred times, repeatedly mulling over the same information. Trying to work through a problem, issue, or creative challenge on your own in this way can only get you so far. Eventually, your mind will run out of ideas, inspiration will stop flowing, and your process will slow down. This is a sign that you've lost your connection with Spirit. You have retreated so far into your own mind that you are no longer present with the larger force.

We often get our best ideas when we're out and about, interacting in the world or doing something we enjoy. Enjoyment is legitimately important. It puts us in a state of flow. This state of flow is what it is to be fully present and engaged—which is the same thing as being connected with Spirit. In fact, this is what it means to be inspired. Interestingly, the words "spirit" and "inspiration" have the same root: the Latin word **spirare**, which means "to breathe." **Inspirare** literally means "to breathe **in** or **blow upon**" or "to infuse (as life) by breathing." Figuratively, "inspire" has come to mean "to influence, move, or guide (as to speech or action) through divine or supernatural agency or power."[1] When we're inspired, we are one with Spirit, and everything comes to us easily. It feels like we're not even working, yet our results are superior to what we could have come up with racking our brains for hours.

---

[1]   Merriam-Webster, "Breathing Life into 'Inspire,'" https://www.merriam-webster.com/words-at-play/the-origins-of-inspire.

We can't rely solely on our minds. We need to also involve our bodies and souls, and the soul of the wider Universe. When we connect them all together through presence, we gain energy and expand our thinking. Perhaps you get up from your desk to get a glass of water. Or you decide to take an early lunch. The next thing you know, you remember an article you read or you bump into a coworker who sparks just the idea you were searching for. It may feel like a coincidence. More advanced spiritual practitioners refer to this as "Synchronicity," which is like a coincidence but implies the presence of a deeper intelligence. While much of Spirit is quiet and invisible, these are **observable** aspects of Spirit at work.

Whatever you want to call it, and whether you assign any meaning to these occurrences, they **are** all happening, regardless of any efforts on our part. But the only way we observe them is if we cultivate our presence.

If you can take the leap into believing that everything is spiritually designed in some mystical way, then you have the opportunity to acknowledge your partnership with the Universe and the motivation to practice presence.

Co-creation

This process of partnering and being present with the Universe is known as "co-creating." Co-creating means:

1. Knowing what you're trying to accomplish and having loose ideas about how you might go about it.

2. Being present and paying attention to feedback from the Universe—acknowledging what you observe as potentially valuable information and being open to its utility.

3. Acting upon it.

If you are a chronic worrier, embracing this partnership will alleviate unnecessary pressure. It will help you refrain from tendencies toward over-responsibility and overthinking.

Let's clear up two common misconceptions about the process of co-creation. The first is the idea that all we have to do is ask for what we want and then sit back, do nothing, and wait for everything to be handed to us. To the contrary, co-creation an active process. The Universe presents clues to us all the time, but it's up to us to pick up on these clues. We can get some uncannily reliable guidance, but it takes work on our part to pay attention, listen, and figure out which impressions are worth following up on.

The second misconception is that these "clues" and "guidance" fall into the mystical realm. What we're really talking about is noticing the regular stuff going on in our lives every day. This simply requires our presence—staying attuned to our own hearts and opening up our five senses. This process connects us to Spirit and our intuition (i.e., gut feelings).

This is why it's called **co**-creation. It is not a form of laziness, stupidity, or shirking responsibility. It is simply a **shifting** of responsibility from your mind to your sensory system, heart, and gut. This is important because your heart and gut know things before your mind catches up with logical understanding. For us goal-minded, action-oriented folks, setting aside our desire to control demonstrates vulnerability and courage.

Let's consider some examples of co-creating with Spirit to help make decisions. When a client of mine, Matt, was contemplating shifting more of his focus from his bread-and-butter business to a side venture he'd been working on, he was excited but nervous. He wasn't sure how he would break the news to his existing partners. I explained the concept of co-creation. He liked the idea but didn't know how to let go of his worries. He continued to fixate.

A couple of months later, his partners approached him to discuss the future of the business. It turned out that they also were thinking about new challenges of their own. After all of his sleepless nights agonizing over what to do, he didn't need to do anything.

Presence teaches us to be rooted in the moment. Matt's desire to find a solution stemmed from his anxiety—and from the fact that he was thinking about a future he couldn't yet know. Presence teaches us to differentiate between what we **think** we need to do and what we **actually** need to do.

Another client of mine, Susie, had been feeling for a long time that she deserved a raise. She kept fretting over how to bring it up with her boss. Obsessed with the specifics of when and how to raise the issue, she kept spinning her wheels over how the meeting would play out.

When we discussed the issue and all of her contributions, she began to recognize what an asset she truly was. She saw that she deserved the raise. Rather than fixate or fret, she made a decision to be brave about standing up for herself. She set an intention to let Spirit lead.

The next time she spoke with her boss, all she told him was that she wanted to meet to revisit her compensation. He asked her to send over a list of all that she had been doing. She had, of course, already created this list, so she was able to send it right away. Within twenty-four hours, he responded via email saying that he hadn't realized how much she had been doing. He offered her a meaningful increase, even making it retroactive. She never even had to meet with him. The meeting she had dreaded and spent hours imagining never took place. By setting her intention and letting go, she allowed Spirit to step in.

Susie didn't mystically let the Universe take control of her life. Rather, she recognized that she had been trying to control the situation, down to how a meeting would play out. When she stopped doing this and made a decision to partner with Spirit, she was in a better position to receive what she wanted. The outcome she desired unfolded with speed, grace, and ease.

To turn to a more personal example, I remember an especially fraught moment for me as a mother. Decision making can be so loaded when our children are at stake, and this certainly holds true when it comes to the topic of breastfeeding. Friends and coworkers of mine have struggled with every aspect of it. Some have had great difficulty doing it. Others have wrestled with how to fit pumping into their work schedules.

My grand plan was to nurse Hannah Grace until her first birthday, just as I had planned to do with Cooper. When she didn't wean on her own by that time, I wondered what to do. I began to fixate on the question. When was she ever going to stop? How long was too long? And if she didn't stop soon, was I going to have to put forth time-consuming and emotionally draining efforts to bring the phase to its end? Then I remembered that I didn't have to answer the question on my own. I remembered that I could trust Spirit to give me a message when it was time. I took the absence of any clear sign or circumstances to mean that it was not time. At least not yet.

Lack of information is, in fact, information. It may not be satisfying, but it reveals the truth. Unless there's an actual deadline, postponing decisions can often be enormously beneficial. Sure enough, months later, I reached a point where I just felt tired of nursing. Seemingly out of nowhere, the joy ran out of it. I sensed my daughter just wasn't into it anymore. *That* was Spirit's guidance. I didn't need to see a medium to interpret the stars. I just needed to pay attention.

That's not to say that weaning my daughter wasn't emotionally challenging. It was quite bittersweet, in fact. But I made the decision with clarity that came from my openness to receive guidance rather than forcing something to happen because of some idea about the way things *should* be.

This approach allowed there to be tenderness and grace between me and Hannah Grace. Whereas before I would have assumed that there was a single, correct course of action, this time, I enjoyed this special phase of babyhood so much more. When we trust Spirit and stay present so we can observe its messages, we find ease in decision making.

Whether we're attempting to co-create with Spirit, to solve a problem, to accomplish a goal, to let go of our worries, or to make an important decision, Spirit will eventually provide what we ask. It will speak through our gut feelings and impressions. The best decisions make themselves known, but only if we tune in to Spirit and remain open and receptive to it.

LESSON 2:
TRUST

*Blind faith is believing what others tell you, but **authentic faith** is trusting your Inner Guidance, a.k.a. intuition, inspiration, instincts, or gut feelings.*

–Scott Noelle

Like presence, trust is a continuation of the concept of Spirit. It's one thing to believe in Spirit, but for those of us who are accustomed to driving results through our own actions, a theoretical belief won't mean much unless we understand how to apply it. This is where trust comes into play. Trust is the bridge between waiting for the Universe to take care of everything on our behalf and taking responsibility for our own lives. You can think of trust as belief in action.

There are two components to trust: **trust in *Spirit*** and **trust in *oneself*** (i.e., one's **higher Self** or **Authentic Self**). ***Trust in Spirit*** entails approaching our lives with the firm belief that Spirit has our back. It means that when we encounter problems, challenges, or opportunities in any area of our lives, we trust Spirit to afford us the thoughts, ideas, information, resources, and solutions we need in order to respond. ***Trust in oneself*** means trusting our own skills, judgment, and track record. Trusting ourselves also means having confidence in our instincts and in our ability to recognize guidance from the Universe.

Trusting in both Spirit and oneself can assist us in knowing that, no matter what happens, we are able to confidently show up for challenges. My own path to trusting Spirit came from a combination of reading and thinking about it and experiencing it firsthand. Time and again, I found myself in situations where I had no choice but to sit back and observe how they unfolded. Each time, without fail, I perceived that listening to Spirit led to clearer and better outcomes than I could have generated through my own will. Reflecting on these experiences was how I cultivated trust.

For example, whenever I've been given group assignments, whether in a job or in graduate school, I often found that the best teams formed by happenstance. A group that came together as a result of whoever happened to sit on either side of me, after a mad dash to find an open seat in a conference room or the classroom, would end up being a stronger team than one I might have selected by design. When I've gone into group assignments determined to work with a certain person, those situations have sometimes backfired. Why? I was trying to exert control and attempting to will the situation into perfection. I was coming from a place of fear rather than one of trust.

When I let go and surrender to a process, I am often amazed—even **awestruck**—by the way everything can fall into place of its own accord and feel so meant to be. During my master's program in spirituality, it became a common refrain in my cohort that no one could have picked a better team by attempting to orchestrate one.

The same was true when it came to determining what material we would explore together. Countless times I began these group sessions with very specific ideas in mind. Then an unforeseen topic would emerge, filled with rich potential for learning and unique to that particular moment and group of individuals. None of us could have known in advance that we shared these common interests, but we could all see that we would be best served by seizing the opportunity presented, even though it would mean we'd need to abandon our original ideas.

"Blindly" sitting wherever we happened to find a vacant chair and surrendering to the flow of the moment proved to be a winning strategy almost every time. Learning can happen in tremendous and entirely unexpected ways when we are fully available to it.

After having this experience over and over again, and hearing from others about similar ones, my understanding began to solidify. I became more willing to trust that everything would work out as it should. This paved the way for me to begin embracing Spirit more willingly as a partner in my life.

From there, I began to find the courage to abandon my tried-and-true methods for tackling challenges in my life and experiment with new ones. It's easier to do things the ways we always have, even if those approaches aren't very effective. But I decided this was a time to make deliberate efforts to rise above my fear. I proceeded like a scientist testing out a hypothesis and observing the results.

I began with low-risk experiments that were only mildly uncomfortable. For example, I might approach a daily problem involving childcare or some minor hassle at work with this new mindset. I built my familiarity slowly over time. The resounding success of these experiments transformed my former, purely intellectual understanding of Spirit into a new way of doing and being in the world. It deepened my understanding of Spirit, allowing my trust to guide me toward successful results.

Trusting Spirit *is a big help in the area of solving problems.* In our culture, we celebrate the power of the mind. I had so much confidence in my cognitive capabilities that I believed I could think my way through any problem using reason and logic. I would analyze and discuss issues from every angle.

Sometimes this compulsive analytical habit would exhaust me from the sheer mental energy involved. When a thought that seemed useful or profound occurred to me—while driving, in the shower, or in the middle of a conversation with a friend—I would hold on to it for dear life. This prevented me from being fully present. I was always distracted, wheels turning.

Eventually I began to learn that important thoughts and ideas would always be there. I could let go. As long as I was willing to relax into a receiving frame of mind, I would consistently cross paths with what I needed. Clues would appear in a dream, through a coincidence or synchronicity, or in a flash. It tended to happen right at the opportune time: when I was poised to apply what came to me. I found that what was truly important and valuable would come back. Oftentimes my thoughts would show up in a clearer, more profound form. Being in a receptive mode was the key to catching them.

As my understanding of the concept of Spirit grew, I even became willing to consider Spirit as the provider of the good ideas and effortless solutions that came to me. This growing belief in Spirit as a wellspring of inspiration created an opening in my consciousness. I became more attuned to its guidance.

The more open I became, the more I improved at noticing and interpreting internal and external information. The ideas, thoughts, answers, and direction that came to me felt as though they weren't coming from *my* mind at all, but rather from the Universal mind. It was as if Spirit had become a part of me, like we had merged. That was when I made the connection that what I had always called "inspiration" was in fact what it meant to be connected with Spirit.

We don't need to rack our brains to solve problems. It's impossible to *run out* of good ideas the way a restaurant might run out of its signature dish—because Spirit is infinite. We don't need to worry about forgetting seemingly important ideas. If we catch a glimpse of an idea at a time when we aren't able to act on it, that just means it flew by us at the wrong moment. It's the same for opportunities. We can't act on everything, and that's okay. We can take comfort in knowing that if something is truly important, it will come back to us. If it's not, we'll get another one that will be equally good, if not better.

When we trust in Spirit and its endless supply of inspiration, we can release our tight grasp and let go of worry. We can receive inspiration anytime we want, simply by being conscious and aware and **ready** to receive it.

Let's look at some specific examples of trusting Spirit. This first one has to do with **trusting Spirit to provide for the highest good.** Years ago, my husband and I applied to some progressive elementary schools in our area for Cooper. It was a time-consuming process that involved quite a bit of soul-searching, and we had to wait several months for the results. We couldn't know for sure where he would get a spot, if he got one at all.

In the past, I would have felt an acute sense that our lives were on hold. This feeling of limbo would have made me too anxious to relax. To mitigate the discomfort of waiting and wondering, I would have wished time away. I would have been desperate to arrive at the date when we would finally learn our fate.

Instead, after sending in applications, we decided to shift our focus to other areas. When we got called in for our interviews, we set our intentions to do the best we could. We attended informational events, but other than that, the process wasn't on my mind. This was a significant contrast with how I previously would have handled those months, obsessing over all the "what-ifs." At the end of the process, when Cooper was admitted to a wonderful school, I was pleased by not only the outcome but also—perhaps more important—the process. I had committed to living in the here and now and enjoying the present. I was more available to my son and my husband. This made me happier than any admissions letter.

All is well. Everything is working out for my highest good. Out of this situation only good will come.

— Louise Hay

Part of trusting the Universe is believing that, even if things don't work out the way we hope, we will grow stronger and wiser. It may take years to make sense of how events shape us, how they really are for our benefit. Even though we may think we know what we want and what's best for us, that is not the case. As the Rolling Stones put it, "You can't always get what you want / But if you try sometime you find / You get what you need."

Part of trusting the Universe involves going deep within ourselves and trusting that we have reliable instincts in place—an inner GPS of sorts—pointing us in the right direction. I realized that my best decisions have come from listening to my gut and that I've generally had a track record of good judgment. I could afford to relax.

At work, for example, I saw that I could follow the flow of my ideas without worrying that I'd get so carried away with one project that I'd miss a deadline on another. When it came time to switch focus, an alert would pop up in my consciousness and I would instinctively shift gears. I didn't need to force it. Enough authentic urgency would be generated to pull my energy and focus where they were required. Contrary to my prior belief, my worrying and obsessing had never been the "X factor" driving my success.

When we are children, we don't have to be told to follow our instincts. Children naturally allow their inner voices to speak. Getting back to that place could be useful to us all. In her book *The Purpose of Your Life*, Carol Adrienne says, "Research shows that most of what we see is something we have already learned. Trust your inner selection process instead of continuing to give energy to confusion, fear, and overcontrol."[2]

A bird sitting on a tree is never afraid of the branch breaking, because its trust is not on the branch but on its own wings. Always believe in yourself.

—unknown

---

2   Carol Adrienne, *The Purpose of Your Life* (William Morrow, 1998), p. 137.

LESSON 3:
ABUNDANCE

*If you look at what you have in life, you'll always
have more. If you look at what you don't have in life,
you'll never have enough.*

–Oprah Winfrey

We all have times when we feel frustrated and unfulfilled.
Struggles of all kinds—whether with our careers, relationships, finances, or broader goals—come and go. At such
junctures, we may walk around feeling burnt out, overwhelmed, exhausted, and desperate, wondering if life
will ever work out. We question why life doesn't square
with our expectations—why we aren't where we thought
we would be, why life isn't giving us what we need.

When I was struggling with my career, when I felt overwhelmed trying to juggle everything and saw the toll my mental state was taking on my family, I didn't know how to create a new reality. I wanted to lead a more empowered and intentional life, to do professional work that was personally meaningful and also participate in more aspects of motherhood. But I was in so deep with my old reality that I didn't have a clue how to get myself out. Recognizing *abundance* in my life was the key that unlocked the door.

What do I mean by abundance? Above all, I am referring to a mindset. Abundance refers to the idea that we already have everything we really need—that it is all within our grasp. This goes beyond money or material desires or achievements. It doesn't mean you already have the house or the job or the relationship you want. It means that you have the means of getting there. This includes personal resources and skills as well as emotional attributes.

An abundant attitude recognizes that the Universe is limitless, with infinite resources. Hence, there is plenty available for all of us. Even when there's something we desire but don't yet have, we have *enough* right now. To feel abundant, we simply need to choose to hold this mindset. We need to change our focus from what's missing to what we already have.

The problem is that it's so tempting and easy to view life from the opposite end of the spectrum. It is more common to encounter a mentality characterized by scarcity, emptiness, dissatisfaction, and lack. We generally think about what we covet: the handbag we want, the car we'd love to drive, the beautiful house on the hill. We look at our friend who has the amazing career, our sibling who seems to have a perfect life, our coworker who looks so put together.

My perception of lack manifested itself as a shortage of trust both in myself and the Universe. I didn't trust in my own talents, relationships, or inner resourcefulness. I believed that *I* wasn't enough, that there was something lacking in my very being. I anticipated scarcity when it came to safety, love, and joy. This bolstered my belief that I had to do everything in my power to build my career, skill set, reputation, and earning power. I was trying to protect myself from future misery. My loyal, faithful, and alarmist ego convinced me, in particular, that I needed a financial cushion. Giving up my income and letting go of the career I had worked so hard to build brought up such palpable fear that it was as if my physical survival were at stake. The thought alone could put a pit in my stomach, make my heart race, and leave me short of breath.

I had wanted to be independent so that I wouldn't have to live on anyone else's terms. But ironically, I was making so many compromises when it came to my needs that I was **already** living on other people's terms. I had been raised to be a people pleaser, and to be particularly accommodating to authority figures. Accordingly, when it came to my boss, I ceded my needs. I regarded her, and all bosses before her, as the ultimate authority figure, and therefore surmised that her requirements were unavoidable, non-negotiable, and beyond my control. I believed I had no choice but to comply.

My spiritual journey revealed that none of my judgments and fears had anything to do with my boss. I realized I was projecting onto her my own insecurities and expectations based on what I had learned and bought into at a young age. I also realized it was unsustainable to go day after day without taking into account what made *me* happy.

I had stumbled into the ultimate paradox: the discontent I was trying to avoid was the very thing making me feel so very disgruntled. I thought that maximizing my income would protect my freedom, but that belief trapped me in the job that felt so unfulfilling. I didn't have the tools to discern how bad it had to get before I could allow myself some mercy. Since I had a pretty thick skin, I kept resisting, believing I could *still* handle it, clutching my "enough is enough" card to save for the *future*, when surely I'd face an even more painful job. I convinced myself that I had no choice. Without realizing it, I had built my own prison.

Opening Our Eyes to Abundance

Because we can't see our blind spots, it makes good sense to bring in an outside perspective. At some point, it occurred to me and my husband that we might not be viewing our circumstances clearly—that where our resources were concerned, we might be making incorrect assumptions based on fear. We had been worrying by default about what it would mean if I left my job. Determined to figure out our options, Marc and I enlisted the help of a financial advisor.

When our advisor gave us a framework for how to think about our finances, we gained clarity about what we needed. To our surprise, our situation wasn't nearly as dire as we had imagined. We would need to find places to cut our spending, but we weren't on the verge of losing our home. We didn't have everything we **wanted**, but we had **enough**. This was our first glimpse of the abundance we had been blind to.

Based on my husband's counsel and some gentle nudging, I came to recognize that I did have a choice. I could go ahead and leave my job. The world wouldn't end. Our budget would be tight, but we wouldn't be homeless. With a deep breath, I decided to do it. It was the first time I chose to prioritize my happiness over protecting myself from my fears.

The unexpected support I received was what finally helped me get to the point of being willing to "cry mercy" and reshape my life. It allowed me to take the leap of faith into the great and uncomfortable unknown. It felt very risky, but I was able to see the **opportunity** in my situation, think more expansively, and find another way. This is a choice we **all** have when we adopt an abundance mindset.

Applying the Lesson of Abundance to Your Life

You might be thinking, "Yeah, sure, quit my job. Easy for her to say!" It's true that not all of us can quit our jobs. I've spoken with single parents, people with unsupportive families, people in all kinds of different situations. What I've learned is that we all possess the tools and skills within us to change our circumstances.

You are more resilient than you know. You are stronger and more talented and more capable than you realize. Fear might be holding you back, telling that you can't possibly move to a new state or change careers or confront a bad relationship. Those fears may come from long-held beliefs that no longer fit your life today.

Even though I now know from personal experience that there are times and circumstances when it may make sense to leave a job without having another one lined up, I recognize that many people don't have this luxury. I would not advocate quitting a job without having some plan in mind for how to pay bills. When change is necessary, it's important to be thoughtful and responsible about **how** we go about making it. This is where the abundance mindset comes into play.

Abundance isn't limited to money. It includes all the resources available to us: our time, energy, creativity, skills, relationships—essentially, anything from which we can derive positive value. The experiences we've accumulated throughout our lives offer a clue about what we can offer the world.

I can't help but think of my friend Lucinda, who got fed up with her corporate life and went on to start her own web design company. This allowed her to earn a living and set her own hours so she could be available to her young family. Then, as her children grew older and the family's needs changed, a steady paycheck became more of a priority. She went back to a corporate job because it suited her needs. And this time she loves it.

Many former colleagues of mine have given up their careers to freelance or start their own businesses. Others have worked temporary assignments while figuring out their next moves. A classmate of mine, Mary, left her well-paying full-time job as an estate manager and began driving for Uber to make money while figuring out what she would do next.

As she describes it, "I really had to embrace my humility. Leaving my job and starting over, as a 42-year-old woman, and with no idea of what I was doing with my life, I had to let go of my ego and the beliefs I was holding around my career. But I knew that I had to do it. I needed to put all my focus on school because my deepest desire was to be in a career that would bring me ultimate JOY!" Through her personal work, she discovered that her real dream was to travel. She eventually got a job as a flight attendant on private jets. She even got to travel with her idol, Stevie Wonder!

Whether you are in a work situation that you know in your heart isn't serving you, in a bad relationship, or dealing with an injury, *fear* should not be the factor that guides your decisions. When fear governs our thinking, it keeps us from allowing for new possibilities. Fear limits us from pursuing a life of happiness. The crucial thing to remember is that, as human beings, we are adaptable. Facing the unknown can be terrifying. Creating change means going against what's comfortable and familiar. But once you do, you'll settle into a new normal. Every person I know who has embraced abundance and made a change reports feeling grateful for it.

LESSON 4:
HUMILITY

*Humility is characterized by a firm understanding
and conviction that God created me just as I am,
with my personality, my strengths and my weaknesses
and that He has a plan for my life.*

–Heather Crawford[3]

One of my favorite coaches, Scott Noelle, says, "Always
remember that embracing humility is empowering, not
humiliating. Humiliation is when humility is forced on you.

---

3   Heather Crawford, "Humility vs. Low Self-Esteem: What Is the
     Difference?" ActiveChristianity, https://activechristianity.org/
     humility-vs-low-self-esteem-difference

When you're already humble, you can't be humiliated." But what does it mean to be humble?

According to the Cambridge dictionary, humility is "the feeling or attitude that you have no special importance that makes you better than others." The key part of this definition is its second half. We are all special—but we are special *equally*.

Humility also involves recognizing that (1) none of us is perfect, (2) we are not nearly as in control of the unfolding of our own lives as we'd like to think, and (3) life is filled with unknowns.

No matter how gifted we are in our own ways, we have weaknesses and limitations. Relative to the Universe, we are powerless. If you think back to the picture I painted in the lesson on Spirit, you'll remember that what we humans control is minuscule in relation to Divine Intelligence. This is the sentiment behind John Lennon's saying that "life is what happens when you're busy making other plans."

We know so very little that we don't even know what we don't know—or why things happen the way they do. Divine Intelligence has plans, methods, and reasons we may never understand. We don't know what the Universe is up to when it doesn't give us what we want. And when we don't feel supported in accomplishing our goals, it's hard not to question what life is up to.

If we choose to take a spiritual perspective, we might wonder what message the Universe has for us, what lessons we're supposed to learn, and whether perhaps we should be doing something different in the larger sense. Being aware that most of the time we have to go through life without knowing the answers to these questions is what it means to be humble.

My journey toward understanding and really experiencing humility began when I embraced the notion that my financial contribution to our family was no longer critical. This turned my entire interpretation of my identity on its head. I'd been telling myself that I was sacrificing my happiness for my family. I'd been thinking that being financially self-sufficient and responsible defined me. My reasons, in fact, had much more to do with my lack of humility. I'd wanted to uphold my self-image, believe that I was central to my family's survival. This—my income—was how I had been assigning myself value.

Shifting to the perspective that we don't have any special importance relative to others can be an uphill battle. Again, this is especially challenging for those of us who are achievement driven. Part of humility is embracing ourselves as we are—without attaching our accomplishments to our identities. After all, our jobs and accomplishments are not what make us valuable or important.

We are each totally unique on this planet, with our own particular blend of talents and perspectives. We also all have our weaknesses—this is part of being human. Understanding this means compassionately accepting our limitations.

So many of us refuse to admit our weaknesses to ourselves. We tell ourselves that we can overcome them. We take an unrealistically harsh and demanding attitude toward ourselves and work ourselves to the bone attempting to "improve"—not recognizing that our weaknesses and flaws don't diminish our ability to be valuable and successful in life.

Allowing ourselves to be human and have humility helps us to focus less on our supposed flaws, thereby freeing up energy that we would otherwise spend attempting to fix them. We create space for our unique gifts to come forward.

There's a tendency to believe that contributions such as being kindhearted and loving are small or minor. They aren't. They matter more than we think. In fact, if our greatest contribution in life were being a consistently good friend or parent, listening to others with genuine caring, or offering a smile or laughter to strangers, that would be wonderful. The world needs more of that.

Once I moved on from my career and began to create distance between it and my self-image, I began to conduct my life much more consciously and authentically. I felt liberated and, at the same time, both peaceful and more enlivened than ever. I felt inner clarity and alignment with my purpose. But then I stumbled upon a frustrating paradox: in discovering my power to be exactly as I was and live according to my own values and priorities, I began to experience my relative lack of power and control in the broader scheme of life.

I thought that eliminating my corporate job responsibilities would free me up. I thought I would have all the time in the world to make fulfilling choices: to take on a project of my choosing, get it done, and move on to the next one. I'd imagined knocking them down one by one, getting to the bottom of my list, and then feeling available to unleash my full potential.

But once I had rid myself of my work obligations, I became flooded with different kinds of obligations. Our family grew. Appliances broke down with alarming regularity, always when I least expected it. I saw that these hassles were a constant. Without a job to obscure this reality, the veil was lifted from in front of the one thing that, for as long as I'd live, I could never get around, and that was life itself. It's one thing to feel resentful of your boss; you can get a new job working for someone else. But you can't escape life. No matter how smart, special, or organized I was, there wasn't much I could do to orchestrate the unfolding of life. That's one thing no human being alive can control.

Acknowledging this, I decided to focus on the one area where I was in charge: my attitude and actions. I generated a new standard for myself: no matter what life threw at me, I vowed to do everything in my power to stay centered and present. I knew this was the key to my ability to return to a state of peacefulness and joy.

In working with clients, I've found that those who are self-employed often struggle with not receiving external validation. From entrepreneurs to artists to small business owners, people who choose to forge their own path have to dig down deep to summon their own determination on a daily basis as they fight off both inner and outer critics and face uncertainty of all kinds. I have come to learn from my own experience that this involves true humility.

From a scientist going out on a limb with an experiment to a schoolteacher attempting to write her first screenplay, in order to pursue their "callings," individuals have to give themselves over to uncertainty as they pursue what can be a scary journey. They must learn to accept that they have to follow a path that reveals just one small step at a time. As the author E.L. Doctorow put it, "Writing is like driving at night in the fog. You can only see as far as your headlights, but you can make the whole trip that way."

During times of uncertainty, it's natural for us want to make things happen by force of will and to try to line everything up to match how we think it should all be. But when we can acknowledge to ourselves that we don't have the answers and don't know how a situation will play out, we actually create a form of knowing—"I have identified something that I am certain I do not know." Scott Noelle calls this being "confidently uncertain."

We can take a moment to recognize that we are facing the great Unknown. Rather than fighting it, we embrace it and refocus our attention on cultivating presence. Being humble in this way shows us what steps we need to take right now.

Humility and Boundaries

Clients often ask me how to establish boundaries. A working mother once said to me, "You know, we cause ourselves so much unnecessary stress because we can't just say *no*. But still, it's so hard to do!" This comes into play for parents who can't bear to see their child cry or face disappointment. It also shows up in the workplace when people take on too much responsibility.

I've observed friends who feel completely overwhelmed and want to pull their hair out because they agreed to take on complex and time-consuming volunteer work—not because the work brought them joy but because they couldn't bring themselves to assert a boundary. I've watched others who feel the need to be perfect—to always have their houses look immaculate or throw a magazine-worthy dinner party. Before they know it, they're hiding in a bathroom stall at work and bawling, or in their therapist's office crumbling under the pressure of it all. Or they get sick or injured from the stress.

This problem is an offshoot of our unwillingness to accept our limitations. We try to do it all because we don't want to let ourselves or others down. We want to be superheroes. Sometimes we say yes, grudgingly, because, without realizing it, we're afraid of diminishing our self-worth. Other times, and often concurrently, we have an inflated view of our own importance and capability. We think we are the *only* ones who can do the job. That's simply not true.

The reality is that everyone has limitations. When we go too long without recognizing this and continue to push ourselves past our limits, we pay the price. There's always an unintended consequence. If we do too much at work, our family suffers. If we do too much for our families, we personally may suffer. If we do too much for our children by removing obstacles in their path, we deny them the opportunity to learn skills they'll need to be well-adjusted and productive adults.

On the flip side, when we admit to ourselves that we can't do it all, and that we aren't required to do so in order to prove our worthiness, we may find it easier to do what's right for ourselves, which is to set limits. When we set limits, we acknowledge our boundaries. Another way to think about it is that when we say no to something, we are actually saying yes to something else. We're creating space for other possibilities to come into our lives. Those possibilities can take various forms. It may be the form of our sanity and well-being. It may be an opportunity to focus on another part of our life—another interest or friendship—or to nurture ourselves physically, mentally, or emotionally. Perhaps the space we create by saying no allows us to rest so that we have more patience for our children. We can't know if we never create that space.

It's easy to believe that when we say no, we're doing something wrong, but that's not the case. What we're doing is caring for ourselves. When we care for ourselves, we enrich our lives. Everyone around us benefits as a result. We also model for our children how to engage in self-care. When we say yes to ourselves, we allow ourselves to be our best in the areas where it counts most.

The reality for most people is that it can be difficult to adopt a humble attitude. Instead of viewing this path as one of self-diminishment, it helps to be open to the idea that *you* alone are not wholly responsible for all your accomplishments. Think back to what we discussed in the lesson on Spirit. Consider how you might begin to shift energetically into an attitude of genuine humility. In the exercise at the end of this book, you'll find tips on how you might try to bring those fears, weaknesses, and limitations out of the shadows and into the light.

Using Meditation to Cultivate Humility

Meditation has recently reemerged as a popular trend. Among many other benefits, meditation is a wonderful way to develop one's sense of humility. The sheer difficulty of something so seemingly simple as sitting in stillness can be an incredibly humbling experience for goal-oriented doers. I realized this one day as I sat in the back corner of my office with my eyes closed, countdown clock running. I wanted to enter into a meditative state, but I noticed how challenging and uncomfortable it was for me to slow down. The experience reminded me that we cannot **make** things happen. At that moment, I could see with crystal clarity that my discomfort was just my ego wanting to have its way. For the first time, I understood that there was nothing in particular meditation needed to be, nor did I need to "get better at it." It was fine for it to be what it was: a practice of sitting still and refraining from any kind of **doing**.

It occurred to me that the practice, particularly in all its discomfort, is a brilliant way to take time, **against the wishes of our results-driven egos**, as a way of acknowledging a force greater than ourselves. It's a time to remember how small we are compared to the whole. If our egos have a hard time sitting still for twenty minutes because they think their contributions are so important that the Universe can't wait, it's a sure sign of an overly inflated view of self.

Rather than fixating on finding the one meditation technique that works best for you, you can try to frame your practice as an invitation for Spirit to work with you. It can be a time to commune with Spirit and attune to its messages while also setting intentions for yourself. This can open up the possibility of experiencing grace and ease in your daily endeavors.

Clients have expressed their concerns to me: "But... what if I have a deadline? I don't have time to meditate." I've certainly felt that way too. However, I also know that our work flows much more effortlessly when we have a calm mind. This is what meditation does for us. Taking even just a few minutes to settle your mind will help you work more efficiently.

Conventional thinking views humility as weakness. But, it is humility that allows the strength to live in the mystery. With humility, I am open to holding my beliefs loosely enough to receive feedback and change course rather than being slavishly attached to my beliefs....

Humility brings appreciation, gratitude, and fulfillment into my life and blesses me with serenity. It is a gift to myself that relieves me of the worry, tension,

*and pain that result from a need to prove something.
Letting go of the need to prove, defend, convince or
be in control allows those close to me to gain more
trust in my caring.*

−Dr. Jordan Paul[4]

---

[4] Dr. Jordan Paul, "With the Strength of Humility Comes
the Gift of Serenity," The Good Men Project, August 31,
2017, https://goodmenproject.com/good-for-the-soul-2/
strength-humility-comes-gift-serenity-bbab/.

LESSON 5:
EGO AND SELF-WORTH

True intelligence is to rise above thinking as a source of all intelligence.

–Eckhart Tolle

Why is it so challenging to accept our weaknesses and limitations? Why are we so uncomfortable when our world feels out of control? Why is it so difficult to have faith in times of uncertainty?

More often than not, the issue is our own egos. Our egos create our suffering. They act out like a scared, frustrated, and overtired child grasping for control in a world it doesn't understand.

But make no mistake; the ego isn't without its merits. After all, it's the part of us that gets stuff done. Without it, we wouldn't accomplish anything. So what exactly is the ego?

Psychologists and theorists have historically defined the ego in varying ways. For example, Freud defined it as a kind of mediator between the primitive and illogical Id (the part of personality that seeks pleasure and tries to avoid pain) and the Super Ego (the conscience and idealized self).[5] In Eastern philosophy, the ego simply refers to one's identity, as in when you say, "I am."

The simplest way to think of the ego is as the part of the mind involving logic and rational thinking. It's responsible for planning and executing all our actions. It also has the crucial job of keeping us comfortable and safe. After all, it's the part of us that's in charge of our survival. Hence, nothing freaks us out, or limits us, like our own egos. Our egos take their jobs so seriously that they'll do everything in their power to attempt to control what happens to us.

But, unfortunately, the ego can get overzealous and wreak all kinds of havoc. It may set off a false alarm if it detects even the slightest hint of a threat. It's like a loyal little puppy, loving you and trying to protect you as best it knows how, but inadvertently making a mess of trouble along the way.

The ego tries to make us believe we are more in control of life's circumstances than we really are. And

---

5   Saul McLeod, "Id, Ego and Superego," SimplyPsychology, 2019, https://www.simplypsychology.org/psyche.html

on the flip side, it will at times convince us that we have *no control* in areas where in fact we do.

The ego is very clever and often shows up in disguise. It tries to trick us into believing our thoughts represent the truth. For example, maybe you have a new love interest or you're interviewing for a job, and you pick up on some familiar red flags. But this time you are convinced the situation is different. Your ego tells you that you should go for the job, pursue the relationship, stay friends with that toxic personality. This is because the ego craves the familiar and wants you to be successful—without thinking that concept through. Your gut, however, may give your ego pause. It may interrupt your ego's messaging, and this moment of pause is always worth heeding.

Before we go believing the commentary presented by our egos, it's important to know that the ego is our smaller self, i.e., our self with a small "s." It's our self-*image*, not our *wise Self* with a capital "S." This small self generates thoughts in a stream of chatter. We listen to the stream of chatter and take it as gospel.

The problem with this is that many of our thoughts are incorrect. They're *mis*interpretations and *mis*understandings. They're often made-up stories and unnecessary judgments based on the past or fears concerning the future—our emotional baggage. When we react to the chatter as if it were true, we create unnecessary drama for ourselves. Without it, we would see experiences in a more neutral and objective light.

Practically speaking, just understanding the ego's role can make it easier to refrain from interpreting its chatter as truth and thereby giving it power over you. This can enable you to see your situation in a different light and from a more expansive point of view, so that you can align your actions with your values and how you want to be in the world.

Perhaps, when faced with the prospect of change, you've had your ego unhelpfully chime in with questions. The ego can sound like this: *What if everything I've ever done in my life has been a colossal mistake? What if I moved to the wrong place and majored in the wrong subject and took the wrong job?* It can also sound like this: *My life looks so different than I thought I would. I'm nowhere close to where I wanted to be. What does that say about me? What if I'm not as impressive or worthy as a person?*

Looking back, I recognize that it was my ego that delayed me in quitting my job. It convinced me with its incessant chatter that doing so would be disastrous. Then, when I went ahead and disregarded its counsel, it served me up an existential crisis replete with unpleasant personal questions. I can see now that my ego's questions were never going to lead me to the purpose and fulfillment I sought. That was because there wasn't actually anything wrong. I was safe and loved, and my life was filled with possibility. I was okay. It was my ego that was having the issue. My ego was uncomfortable. It ran around my brain, hitting the panic button and sounding the alarm.

The issues I sought to resolve through all of my mental machinations were like shadow puppets. My ego perceived them, but they weren't real. With the flip of a switch, an overhead light could have made them disappear. At the time, I couldn't locate the switch. I fumbled in the dark, searching for answers to dispel those looming figures.

Recognizing the Ego

When it comes to personal matters, the ego's logic can get so mixed up with fear that it becomes illogical. It can ask us to buy into misguided beliefs. It coaxes us into thinking it's keeping us safe, all the while creating a sort of mental prison.

We need to listen to our thoughts and ask if we're hearing our wise *Self* or the ego's chatter. The voice of your wise Self feels like it's coming from your gut or your core, while the ego's chatter takes place between your ears. Your wise Self speaks more slowly, while the ego yips away at high volume and speed.

As you observe your thoughts, try to recognize their source. Unless what you're hearing feels calm, like unfaltering inner knowing, genuine enthusiasm, or any of the other hallmarks of Spirit that we've discussed, understand that you do not need to placate it with answers. Instead, try to remember that what you're hearing is simply your fear-driven ego sensing a threat and hitting the panic button—just as it's designed to do. While it may be true that a small piece of your ego is being destroyed, your authentic self will be safe and intact. We have nothing to fear. The trick is to recognize chatter for what it is.

Self-Worth

A central issue that arises from the ego is questioning our **self-worth**. Related to the question "Who am I?" are the questions "How *worthwhile* and *valuable* am I?" and "Am I *enough*?" Our level of fulfillment is tied to the degree to which we are able to express who we are in the world through our contributions.

Often, deep down, we don't feel good enough. This can manifest in different ways. It can come out through self-deprecating humor or flattery of others. We've all had that gushy friend who says things like "You're so amazing, I'm not even worthy of being in your presence!" She may not realize she has issues with her self-worth; she may simply think she's giving an honest compliment. But when statements like this are a pattern, we must examine them.

Worth often comes disguised as something else entirely. In the moment, we may not feel insecure. Instead we might feel nervous, frustrated, or jealous. It's when we dig deeper that we find the root of our emotions. For example, imagine the case of someone who keeps making poor choices in his romantic relationships. Over and over, he dates the wrong sort of person. He attracts women who bring all kinds of emotional drama to the relationship. It seems like there are always major challenges the woman is attempting to overcome—familial discord, physical or mental health issues, financial trouble. And he's always coming to her rescue.

On the surface, he may just look unlucky. But if he were to dig into his past, he might recall that his own mother was constantly in trouble. If he thought about it further, he might find that she leaned on him and relied on him. Over time, he unconsciously began to associate selflessness with being loved. He may have concluded that if he wasn't in the process of saving someone, he wasn't valuable. A pattern was formed—one that no longer serves him as an adult seeking equal partnership.

In my life, one consistent hang-up was the feeling that I had to be unquestionably credible in order to be trustworthy. It made me afraid to speak up, and I was consumed with an obsessive need to educate myself. In school and at work, I preferred to present my thoughts and ideas in written form so that I could provide triple-checked information. I didn't trust that I could communicate accurately in the moment. I didn't think my opinions could be trustworthy unless I could defend them. In other words, I didn't feel like *I* was enough.

In both cases, issues with self-worth cause the ego to chatter away. Our poor bachelor doesn't listen to his gut when he sees red flags on a date. His ego blathers away: **This time will be different! Perhaps this woman is the one!** In my case, I didn't trust myself or listen to my inner voice. I allowed my frantic ego to take over, telling me to prep more, study more, read more. The ego floats endless worst-case scenarios, a voice of doom and fear: **If you don't date this woman, you might end up alone!** or, **If you don't study and prepare, you're just goofing off, and then you won't get anywhere in life!**

Chatter like this often occurs far beneath the surface of our conscious awareness. The ego speaks in a whisper. Yet it still powerfully affects our daily lives and our emotional experience.

When we feel unworthy, we may turn on ourselves—or on others. Perhaps you know someone who always feels the need to correct people around her. She can't let someone's error slip by unnoticed. She gives unsolicited advice and feels compelled to offer solutions, even if someone makes clear they simply want to vent. Such a person may not come across as insecure. She may seem brash or patronizing. But her insecurities are what causes her to be so vocal. This is a form of defensiveness. If someone's self-worth is low, they have to constantly justify their own existence and ways of thinking. Their ego feels constantly threatened. They can't simply sit back and listen. They can't create space for others without feeling under personal assault.

When we feel worthy, we are able to self-advocate. We understand that support—whether physical, mental, emotional, or spiritual—has nothing to do with our value. For many people, self-advocacy can feel scary or indulgent. We don't give ourselves permission to nurture ourselves.

In our culture of chronic stress, we see examples of this all the time. Perhaps you know someone who deals with constant pain. Perhaps that person is you. We sit at our desks for epic stretches, then take breaks only to get lost in our phones. When I was in grad school, I had debilitating back pain. I noticed that some of my classmates sat in reclining chairs at the back of the room. But even though it occurred to me to inquire about reserving one myself, I struggled to *allow* myself to do this. I wondered if my need was legitimate. I questioned whether my back hurt *enough* for special treatment. Would I be taking up a chair someone else needed more than I did? I feared how others would perceive me—that they would think I was faking it. Even if the chair was more physically comfortable, the prospect of drawing attention to myself was emotionally uncomfortable.

We should never suffer physically, yet so many people do. Perhaps we know we should take better care of ourselves—get up and take breaks, exercise more, seek help—yet we don't allow ourselves to do so. We might tell ourselves our pain is not so bad. But when is pain ever okay?

We don't need to suffer to be worthy of assistance. We can take care of ourselves *just because*.

Self-advocacy and self-worth mean recognizing and honoring how we feel—no matter the severity of it. If something is good for you, if it will help you, that is justification enough. This is a question of worth only if we make it one. It doesn't have to be that way.

Recognizing our inherent worth is beneficial not just for ourselves, but for those around us. When we approach our lives from the perspective that we are undeniably worthy, it translates into self-love, which directly affects the energy we can contribute back to the world and to our community.

In this interconnected universe, every improvement we make in our private world improves the world at large for everyone. We all float on the collective level of consciousness of mankind so that any increment we add comes back to us. We all add to our common buoyancy by our efforts to benefit life…. It is a scientific fact that "what is good for you is good for me."

—David Hawkins[6]

---

[6]   Dr. David R. Hawkins, *Power vs. Force*, revised ed. (Carlsbad, CA: Hay House, 2012), p. 132.

LESSON 6:
GRATITUDE

Being in a state of gratitude actually creates magnetism, and of course, a magnet draws things to itself. By giving authentic thanks for all the good you now have, as well as the challenges, through this magnetism you'll start the flow of more good into your life.

—Wayne Dyer[7]

Gratitude is a beautiful, life-transforming quality that can expand our experience of joy in life. Recognizing and being grateful for our blessings is instrumental in fueling self-worth, connecting with Spirit, and quieting the ego's chatter.

---

[7]   Wayne Dyer, *The Power of Intention* (Hay House, 2010), p. 130.

When we practice gratitude, we broaden beyond the scope of self-worth, layering in elements of happiness and well-being. Our joy becomes infused with conscious awareness. Rather than waiting for it to arrive, we cultivate it. Gratitude thus becomes a kind of practice.

In the past, when things were going well for me, I would worry that my good fortune was unjust. I wanted good fortune to be equitable among all people. Meeting with success tended to make me uncomfortable, which would detract from the positivity of my experience. I never allowed myself to celebrate. Then I learned to shift my mindset to one of gratitude.

When life is going well, it is crucial that we pause and appreciate our blessings. The reality is that good fortune is impermanent. Life isn't always smooth sailing. We're not always happy or healthy or getting along with our loved ones. Stressful events crop up and can pose serious obstacles to our well-being. For that very reason, when things are going well, it's important to appreciate the moment. As the saying goes, "Get it while the getting's good." We must soak it all in while we can.

Many people find it helpful to make a list of things in their life for which they are grateful. It's beneficial to make this a regular practice. You may find it useful to keep an ongoing list that you add to, or you can simply jot down what you are grateful for on a given day. Your list might include particular relationships (family, friends, partners) or your surroundings (your home, your town or city, your work environment). It can also include small details. Perhaps you're grateful for an interaction with a kind neighbor or the funny text you received from a cherished friend. Maybe you had an endearing moment with your child or spouse, or you did something at work that felt good. Maybe a primo parking spot opened up just as you were approaching your destination.

I have reached a point where I'm grateful for just about everything. In addition to what we feel grateful for on a daily basis, it can also be helpful to express gratitude for our circumstances—both positive and negative.

For example, many people report that the end of a long relationship or marriage can open the door to gratitude. The circumstances may start off as quite negative and painful: being dumped, discovering a spouse was having an affair, realizing the relationship has lost its spark. Yet that pain creates opportunities for soul-searching. The person becomes stronger, more self-aware, more in touch with her needs, and ends up marrying a better partner. This is gratitude in its deepest form: the ability to recognize the opportunity and growth wrought by heartbreak, an idea we'll come back to in the next section (Gratitude 2.0).

The concept of gratitude has been so powerful in my own life that my family has incorporated it into our weekly routine. Every Sunday night at dinner, we each share three things from the week for which we are grateful. It has become a special way to connect as a family and be mindful of our blessings.

To demonstrate the benefit of gratitude very tangibly, I'll share this story. One evening, our family was walking home from a restaurant. Since it was late, we decided to get started on our "gratitudes" while we walked, rather than waiting until we got home. Cooper, who was four at the time, was tired and grumpy. He whined that he didn't want to do it.

So I began with things I knew he had enjoyed over the weekend—going to the park, eating an ice cream cone. The moment the words came out of my mouth, Cooper jumped in with an enthusiastic "Yeah!" He spontaneously went on a roll, recalling all the fun things we had done. In a matter of seconds his mood went from foul to fantastic. He was able to see for himself that when we focus on what we're grateful for, we stay anchored in a positive frame of mind. Life feels a whole lot better.

Over the years it has been beautiful to witness our son authentically express his appreciation for what he has. I'll also never forget the time when I found Hannah Grace, at age two and a half, in the laundry room throwing hats all around and laughing. When she saw me standing there, she looked up at me and said, "I'm grateful to laugh!" We'd had no idea she knew the meaning of the word.

The key to gratitude is authenticity. It's not about pointing to things that **should** make you happy or trying to force a positive attitude. Nor is it about denying the reality of the parts of your life that don't align with your values, priorities, and preferences. The goal is not to come up with a bunch of reasons to convince yourself to be happy. In fact, we have to be careful not to use gratitude as a form of denial. When I was miserable in my job, I attempted to convince myself to be happy by trying to focus on the positive aspects: my short commute, easy parking, and my fantastic coworkers. It was just a weak effort to mask all the ways I was deeply unhappy.

The purpose of a gratitude practice is to help you reflect on the parts of your life that **authentically** improve your daily existence by adding joy or meaning. It's about raising awareness of the sources of pleasure in your life. The goal is to awaken your senses so you can more fully extract value from what's **already** present in your life. It's about maximizing your mindshare of good feelings and bringing joy back into the moment.

Gratitude 2.0

Each negative feeling can actually be considered a spiritual opportunity to work with it and possibly heal or resolve it for the very last time.

—H. Ronald Hulnick and Mary R. Hulnick[8]

As we flex our gratitude muscle and build it, we can level up in our practice. This next lesson is challenging. It doesn't come easily or intuitively. It involves looking at experiences that appear to be negative and finding a way to not just accept them but feel authentic gratitude for them. It entails finding opportunity in crisis. This practice, which we can think of as Gratitude 2.0, consists of discovering life's hidden gifts. It means understanding that our richest

---

[8]   H. Ronald Hulnick and Mary R. Hulnick, *Loyalty to Your Soul* (Hay House, 2010), p. 95.

and most rewarding opportunities come not when things go our way—but when we're faced with difficulty.

When I was first introduced to the concept of finding the gifts in suffering, it wasn't hard to grasp on a theoretical level. But as I reflected on my most painful memories, I wasn't sure I could identify any tangible benefits. So I tucked the idea in my pocket while remaining open to discovering how it might apply in my life. I hoped that if I let it percolate in the back of my mind, the answers would eventually reveal themselves.

Sure enough, one day I was working as a facilitator to my classmate Claire, supporting her as she explored her feelings about her sister and parents. According to Claire, her sister had failed to become a self-sufficient and emotionally mature grown-up, despite being in her sixties. Meanwhile, Claire had managed to achieve terrific success in her career while also having a fulfilling marriage and family life. Nonetheless, her parents regularly heaped praise on the sister, giving Claire no recognition whatsoever for her accomplishments. She was filled with sadness and resentment.

In the final minutes of our session, everything seemed to come together for her, resulting in a profound epiphany. She realized that what she perceived to be a lack of validation from her family was really just a mirror being held in front of her, reflecting back her **own** inability to validate **herself.** Witnessing the emergence of her insight gave me a deep sense of contentment for her.

In that moment, it occurred to me that certain types of experiences seem to keep showing up in our lives, as if they're meant to teach us an important lesson—a lesson tailored specifically to us. The more difficult to stomach, the greater its potential to teach us something that can transform our lives for the better.

Like Claire, I had often struggled with feeling unrecognized for my contributions. Whenever I thought about it, I too felt sadness and resentment. And just like Claire, I had an *aha!* moment when I realized that this painful, recurring feeling had little to do with other people. The issue was inside me. What had seemed like an injustice ("Why don't I ever receive validation?") now struck me as opportunity ("What if I can validate myself and know intrinsically that I am enough?"). I saw the hidden gift.

In a nearly mystical way, I saw that, until I learned to resolve this issue within myself, I'd continue to attract similar situations into my life. Specifically, until I learned to validate *myself*, I would probably continue to find myself in situations where I felt underappreciated.

Upon internalizing this new insight, I felt not only exhilarated but also empowered. The feeling I longed for was within my control. I suddenly felt profoundly grateful for those negative experiences. I realized that if I had continually received praise, I might have come to rely on that external feedback to know my self-worth. I might never have known how to foster it internally. This insight was truly a blessing.

Once I saw that, I stopped even craving the external recognition. As Steven Covey says, "Difficult circumstances often create paradigm shifts, whole new frames of reference by which people see the world and themselves and others in it, and what life is asking of them.

Their larger perspective reflects the attitudinal values that lift and inspire us all."[9]

Gratitude 2.0 freed me from my habit of replaying negative events in my head and rehashing them to process why I was so upset. By reframing negative issues as blessings, we open the door to learning. We see that we are not victims of random events, nor are we strangely unlucky. Recurring circumstances serve a purpose. They are gifts designed to teach us important lessons that benefit us over the long run. These gifts, however, do not come wrapped in shiny paper.

We all know that painful experiences can be our best teachers. As the German philosopher Friedrich Nietzsche put it, "That which doesn't kill us makes us stronger." Some say the Universe specifically designs and orchestrates individual lessons to help us advance. Others say it is our choice to view challenges as opportunities. Either way, everything that happens to us can be used for our learning. When we can view life accordingly, we have truly mastered gratitude.

---

[9] Stephen Covey, *The 7 Habits of Highly Effective People* (Simon & Schuster, 1994), p. 75.

LESSON 7:
EMOTIONS

*Your intellect may be confused, but your
emotions will never lie to you.*

—Roger Ebert

Sometimes when we experience especially painful moments, we're not yet ready or able to feel grateful or to process a lesson. Wisdom and clarity can feel a long way off, and we have no choice but to sit with difficulty. So how do we endure such painful moments? Whether it's grief, disappointment, heartbreak, or failure, what tools are available to help us cope?

Perhaps one of the most counterintuitive lessons is to give in to our feelings. When feelings are negative, the human tendency is to resist or repress them. If you feel rejected or betrayed, if you are in the midst of loss or pain, you may seek distraction. It comes in many forms: alcohol, food, the internet, retail therapy, sex, television. We try to numb our pain. We recoil from discomfort. This is common and understandable.

Growing up, I was taught to either repress negative feelings or find the positive. I became a master of compartmentalization and distraction. When faced with stress, worry, or controversy at the office, I slapped on a happy face and socialized with my coworkers. I deflected discomfort with humor. I focused on my work. But in my master's program, in all the classes I was taking, the books I was reading, the work I was doing, I heard again and again that feelings weren't to be eschewed or glossed over. I saw that I didn't need to make my feelings go away at all. The best thing I could do to support myself while experiencing challenging emotions was to acknowledge their presence.

As it turns out, accepting feelings as they are, rather than resisting them, helps negative feelings diminish more quickly. As Dr. Lissa Rankin says, "Emotions are just like labor contractions. They move through you as an energy form. If you resist them, they hurt more, but if you just soften into them, they pass in waves."[10] It is difficult to accept pain, but we need to respond to ourselves with loving compassion, just as we would to a friend.

---

[10]   Dr. Lissa Rankin, "5 Steps to Letting Go of Your Victim Story," Chopra Center, April 28, 2016, https://chopra.com/articles/5-steps-to-letting-go-of-your-victim-story.

We can let thoughts rush through our heads as feelings arise, but we don't have much to gain from arguing with our feelings. We're best served by choosing instead to observe our emotions and then let them go. When we let feelings pass through us and arrive without judgment, a new understanding or awareness eventually follows. Soon enough, we end up feeling better.

There's no such thing as one objective truth when it comes to why we struggle. More often than not, there are many different, simultaneous, and contradictory truths. Searching for the *real* truth or trying to figure it all out rationally can cause a lot of anxiety with very little, if any, return on the energy investment.

When you find yourself stuck in this sort of loop, it's a sure sign that you need to step outside your cognitive rut. When I say "step outside," I'm not suggesting you avoid the issue or pretend it doesn't exist. I'm talking about using techniques on one of the other three levels of consciousness—physical, emotional, and spiritual—to resolve whatever issue is upsetting you. As Albert Einstein said, "No problem can be solved from the same level of consciousness that created it."

Thinking is not the best way to resolve difficult emotionally based problems. We can't think our way out of feelings. We just have to feel. This conclusion is the polar opposite of what I'd believed my whole life. But I now know that thinking can be overrated. Sometimes we simply need to allow our emotions to light the way.

It appears that our inner world is continually up to something we know nothing about, unless we shut off the outer stimuli. Or another question, another possible aspect for exploration: Is it possible for the whole body, the whole organism, to learn something that the mind does not know or only learns later?

—Carl Rogers[11]

A number of techniques can help us when we feel emotionally raw. We're hearing a lot these days about the effectiveness of meditation and mindfulness, which we discussed in the lesson on humility. These techniques can be very effective in helping us create space to release stress and regain equilibrium. Many people also report feeling calmer and experiencing clarity and inspiration while hiking, jogging, or simply taking a shower. Activities like these enable us to commune with nature and connect with ourselves and Spirit in a way that can bring us peace. The reason is that engaging in these activities gets you **out of your head**.

Another technique that serves this purpose is free-form writing. Also referred to as "stream-of-consciousness writing," this technique allows us to bypass our minds and let our underlying feelings come forward uncensored and untainted by our thoughts. In my experience, the physical act of scribbling on a page typically reveals that my situation is far less complex than it seemed when my

---

11   Carl Rogers, *A Way of Being* (Mariner Books, 1995), p. 313.

thoughts about it were swirling around in my head with nowhere to go.

Free-form writing is like a sieve for your emotions. The act of downloading everything in your awareness onto paper is like sifting for gemstones. Amidst all the noise and filler of various thoughts, you can spot your feelings, glittering on the page. They stand out. **Aha!** you think. **There you are.** Free-form writing allows you to separate the valuable emotional nuggets from your thought sediment. Once you filter your emotions out of the muck, everything becomes a lot less complicated.

Many people resist free-form writing because it strikes them as silly or pointless. I used to resist it because I believed I didn't have time for anything that wasn't directly related to my goals and responsibilities. I assumed the exercise would be onerous. But I found that every moment I spent getting my thoughts down on paper and out of my head turned out to be time well spent.

I still sometimes catch myself slipping into my old habit of dealing with confusion by trying to analyze and sort out my thoughts. But when I have the wherewithal to stop and free-form write instead, I quickly discover my raw emotions—fear, hurt, anger. In doing so, I am reminded that we don't necessarily need to understand our thoughts. We just need to **give our feelings a voice** so that we can release them.

When sitting down for a stream-of-consciousness exercise, ask yourself what you **feel** in the moment. Then let your pen go, without judging whatever comes out. If you get stuck, you might give yourself some prompts: "Right now, in this moment, I feel…" Or you can identify sensations in your body: "I have tension in my neck" or "I feel constriction in my throat." Allow yourself to give voice to **whatever** arises. It doesn't matter if it sounds smart, if it's a complete thought, or if it makes any sense at all. Emotions don't need to make sense. Just let them all come out.

You will find that emotions provide you with important guidance. The reason is that they don't lie. There's nothing truer than emotions. Think about it: you can change your mind, but when's the last time you successfully changed how you felt? As much as we may wish at times that we could, we can't convince our emotions to be different than they are.

As Daniel Gilbert, author of **Stumbling on Happiness**, says, "Your emotions are meant to fluctuate, just like your blood pressure.... It's a system that's supposed to move back and forth, between happy and unhappy. That's how the system guides you through the world."[12] When we don't recognize and give voice to our emotions, we run the risk of being driven by them without even knowing it, leading us to make irrational decisions. We're in a huff, feeling self-righteous, and shoving some point of view down someone else's throat—or our own.

When we do take the time to listen to our emotions, we gain a much better idea of what's really going on and

---

[12]   Daniel Gilbert, interview by Andrea Sachs, "Happiness Is...," *Time*, May 3, 2006, http://content.time.com/time/arts/article/0,8599,1190379,00.html.

what's important to us. Listening clarifies our needs. The desire to be logical often drives us to push our emotions away—but embracing them and making space for them to be heard is what actually loosens their grip on us. It frees us to arrive at a calm place of clarity. That's the logic we're seeking.

Unexpressed emotions will never die. They are buried alive and will come forth later in uglier ways.

–Sigmund Freud

LESSON 8:
RESPONSIBILITY

Look at the word responsibility—
"response-ability"—the ability to choose your
response. Highly proactive people recognize that
responsibility. They do not blame circumstances,
conditions, or conditioning for their behavior.

–Stephen Covey[13]

In our discussion about humility and Spirit, we explored how we are not as in control of our lives as we would sometimes like to believe. Yet we do have a great deal of responsibility. Accepting this premise—and keeping

---

[13] Stephen Covey, *The 7 Habits of Highly Effective People* (Simon & Schuster, 1994), p. 71.

it top of mind throughout life's ups and downs—can be one of the most empowering tools available to us.

Let's look at how we can apply responsibility. It comes down to two main ideas: (1) ownership and (2) choice. Ownership suggests that our thoughts, actions, and emotions fall within our own domain. Choice refers to the fact that everything we think, say, and do comes from a decision we've made. We've already touched upon how we can invite more positive emotion into our lives through gratitude. In this lesson, I'll focus on how we can use ownership and choice to work through *unpleasant* emotions—and how embracing that ownership can empower us.

In life, we are subject to an ongoing flow of circumstances, both good and bad. When we get swept up in something that leads us to feel hurt, angry, sad, frustrated, or afraid, it's easy to lose our cool and blame someone or something outside ourselves. Some of us like to blame "the system," or we might feel as though forces are conspiring against us.

The problem is that when we place blame externally, we inadvertently position ourselves as victims, rendering ourselves powerless. We cannot by force of will make another person change their behavior or worldview. Nor can we change reality. If you get stuck in unexpected traffic when you're already late, there's nothing you can do about all the vehicles on the road. If your internet connection keeps failing, you have to spend your time dealing with it, even if you're cramming to meet a deadline. These are facts of life. Your anger at the other drivers or the cable company won't fix the problem.

On the other hand, when we reflect inward in search of our own responsibility, we can empower ourselves to do something positive and productive. You might ask, "How could I possibly assume responsibility for something outside of my control?" The answer is that while we may not be responsible for what has occurred, we are responsible for our *internal* reactions and responses.

You might be thinking, *Ali, didn't you* just **tell us a few pages ago that we can't control our feelings?** Well, yes. And no. Our feelings are our feelings. We can't make them disappear by pushing them away. However, because our emotions arise from our thoughts about what's going on in our lives, we can *direct* them by shifting our beliefs and interpretations of events. By being conscious and intentional about the way we frame an experience, we can find more peace in the moment. We can change our mindset about such incidents and modify our behavior patterns to avoid putting ourselves in future crises. This is how we embrace our own agency and how responsibility empowers us.

Responsibility involves heeding our emotional guidance system for the opportunities it offers. It means revising our beliefs and examining our patterns. When we embrace responsibility, we ask ourselves why we're upset. We attempt to identify why a situation is disturbing to us.

Oftentimes the reason involves the past. Something that happened a long time ago threatened our sense of safety or well-being, and we decided on the spot how we would respond to protect ourselves in similar situations going forward. For example, a client once shared how anxious she became over the question of what to wear whenever she had an important meeting. Her anxiety struck her as disproportionate to the situation. She didn't want to be so fixated on her appearance. She knew rationally that whatever she wore would be fine—yet there she was, an intelligent, capable woman, reduced to tears as she stood before her closet.

It turned out that her mom, who had always been glamorous, used to criticize her appearance when she was a girl. She felt her mother's disapproval acutely. She internalized the message that if she didn't look just right, she would never be taken seriously. This insecurity persisted and came out whenever she had an important meeting. It was an opportunity to shine professionally, but she feared her appearance would cost her the recognition she deserved.

Reflecting on the situation, my client recognized the source of her anxiety. She allowed herself to feel anger and hurt on behalf of her childhood self, and she could then let go of those emotions. She was able to move beyond blaming her mother. She recognized that she had an opportunity to reframe her experience and update her beliefs based on what she valued, and soon enough she no longer felt paralyzed by wardrobe decisions.

In fact, months later, when the woman met her mother for lunch and the first words out of her mouth were "Honey, look at how long your hair is!" the woman had an epiphany. In the past, she would have interpreted her mother's comment as a criticism. She would have sat there, silently fuming, convinced her mother was at it again. But now she recognized that her mother's comment was actually benign. "I was the one supplying the interpretation," she marveled. "I was the one doing the criticizing!"

Certain kinds of experiences become triggers for us, activating memories and patterns automatically, without our realizing it. Everyone has some area in his or her life that creates issues. This applies even to people who always appear cool, calm, and collected on the outside. When you take ownership of your interpretation of events, you make room to draw a different conclusion. You get to *choose* a more supportive and nurturing one. Maybe it's "I like my hair, and I'm glad that as a grown-up I can make choices about how I look." Or maybe it's "I see my mother's comment in a new light, recognize our old pattern, and feel compassion for her."

When we embrace responsibility, we redirect our emotions without dismissing them. Typically, when we remove the dissonance between our ego's anger- and fear-driven thoughts and the truth according to our more elevated and evolved authentic selves, we feel better. We get clearer about who we want to be. We foster gratitude and self-love. This is the power of responsibility.

Something to keep in mind is that potentially upsetting things happen all the time, but things that upset one person don't even register for someone else. This is because, while we all have vulnerable areas, our triggers are different. I used to think that some people were just unusually lucky for having the ability to remain calm in any kind of storm. I've since learned that those people had their own issues; I was just observing them in situations that weren't problematic for them.

Responsibility shows us why we can never accurately say that someone else is causing us to become upset. We only become upset if the situation is something that is **already** an issue for us, bringing up a feeling that already resides within us. The only way to work with that emotion is to take responsibility for it.

Over time, we can learn to recognize our triggers more readily. We begin to notice how each new experience comes packaged in its own unique context. We become more mindful when our emotional response system is activated. Most of the time, we'll discover that there's no verifiable threat to our present safety.

Once we have the wherewithal to see that, we can begin to reap the benefits of processing our emotions through the lens of responsibility. Our job is first to name the emotion that surfaced. We then try to recall any past situation(s) that might be relevant. As in my client's example, you may have thought you were angry about one thing when, in fact, you were responding to something from long ago.

When you can recognize the original source of your emotion, you can work through your feelings. You can forgive yourself for taking on beliefs meant to protect you way back when—as a child dependent on others—and recognize where you are today. This will also give you more clarity to help you resolve problems and clear up misunderstandings with others. You'll be able to make a new choice that suits the situation at hand.

Simply remembering that we are in charge of our thoughts and behaviors can be such a useful tool. It slows us down so we can create space between what happened and what we say or do next. We step outside our current frame of reference and look at the situation from a higher altitude. This calms us down. We observe our feelings before reacting. We discover solutions we couldn't see from ground level and come up with different ways of responding.

Choosing a healthier alternative can be much harder to do; exercising self-restraint may not feel as satisfying in the moment as expressing rage. But it is possible. Knowing we have choice empowers us to work through our emotions in productive ways that won't damage our relationships—for instance, writing them down, going for a walk, discussing them with a confidant or professional, or simply taking a moment to center ourselves. Instead of getting angry, feeling sorry for ourselves, and complaining to everyone who will listen, we can take positive action. When we do respond, we can do so purposefully, with clarity and care. We preserve the sanctity of our relationships, reinforce emotional trust, and do a better job dealing with the situation.

An important way we can create space to examine our choices is by reflecting on our triggers. If you find yourself annoyed when your child takes forever to put on socks and shoes, ask why that might be. Are you afraid of being late? Do you feel hurt by the perception that you're being disrespected? Were you given enough time and space to get ready when you were a child? What judgments do you hold against yourself when you're running late? In many cases, the reason behind our annoyance goes deeper. It isn't really about the getting dressed and out the door.

The reason it's so important to recognize all of this comes back to the idea of ownership. Blaming our feelings on our children's behavior doesn't help us feel better. In fact, it may make us feel worse—and our children suffer the consequences. The same applies to our spouses, partners, and colleagues. On the other hand, when we recognize that how we feel is related to what's going on inside us, we make adjustments. We can remove our own emotions from the equation and work with them separately as we focus on becoming better problem solvers in the situation at hand.

As Stephen Covey notes in The 7 Habits of Highly Effective People, "The place to begin any relationship is inside ourselves." He continues, "As we become independent, we then can choose to become interdependent—capable of building rich, enduring, highly productive relationships with other people."[14]

Reacting vs. Responding

By applying responsibility, we can separate our emotional response from the demands of the situation to

---

[14]   Stephen Covey, The 7 Habits of Highly Effective People (Simon & Schuster, 1994), p. 187.

create better outcomes. This process means the difference between feeling like a helpless victim and feeling
empowered. And isn't this what we all want—to feel like
we're **in charge** of our lives?

We've all heard people tell about an upsetting situation and how they handled it. They'll say, "The thing is, I
had no other choice." But it's not true that we don't have
choices. Life is always filled with options. Just because
we don't like the ones we see doesn't mean they don't
exist. **Everything** is a choice. We are always choosing one
way over another. Recognizing this truth is the way we
take responsibility for our thoughts.

The problem with telling ourselves we don't have
choices is that we end up going in one of two directions—both undesirable. Either we have an emotionally
driven and **misguided** knee-jerk reaction that may cause
collateral damage, or we respond in a virtuous way but
feel like a victim. If similar situations occur repeatedly,
we'll build resentment.

Oftentimes our belief that there's only one acceptable
option is really just a reflection of our value system. So
we would actually deserve credit for making an excellent choice that demonstrates personal integrity! But
it's difficult to give ourselves positive acknowledgment
when we feel that our arm has been twisted. This is why
what's important is **how** we arrive at our decisions.

To apply the concept of responsibility to your life
requires understanding the difference between **reacting**
and **responding**. **Reactions** are automatic, unconscious, and
emotional. They can lead to bad decisions that stymie

our goals and damage relationships with ourselves and others. *Responses* come from a place of equanimity. We are aware of our power to choose what we think, say, and do. We're cognizant of the fact that what's being asked of us is simply *to make a choice*. Therefore, we do so with consciousness and intention.

When we approach challenging situations by taking a step back, considering our options, and proactively choosing how we will respond, we give ourselves the opportunity to align our thoughts, beliefs, and values with our circumstances.

The Power of Language and Visualizing Our Goals

Finally, let's talk about the concept of responsibility as it relates to manifesting our goals. Whether we're speaking out loud or thinking silently to ourselves in the form of self-talk, our words are powerful. The words that form our thoughts create our reality. They get captured in our bodies as feelings and then influence how we interpret the events around us and the choices we make. As Buddha famously said, "What you think, you become. What you feel, you attract. What you imagine, you create." Hence, if we want to achieve our goals, it's important that we hold ourselves accountable for the message we tell ourselves.

Language behaves as intention. Whatever we say, even in jest, we begin to believe. The more frequently we speak or think certain words to ourselves, the more deeply we'll believe them and act accordingly. This is why we should be impeccable with the words we choose. We are best served by using words that are specific, accurate, and positive.

The difficulty is that so much of our language is unconscious and habitual. As we discussed in the lesson on ego, the mind can be a noisy place, filled with chatter on a loop. This creates internalized messages about who we are that may or may not be accurate—or supportive. We adopt language from the messaging we heard during our upbringing. As adults, we absorb messages from the people around us. Have you ever noticed the way roommates and colleagues start using the same phrases? Even our accents and intonation can blend with others'. Oftentimes our words are harmless, but when they're personal and relate to things that matter deeply to us, they can have a lasting effect.

Negative language, including seemingly innocuous sarcasm, can project into our future and block us from achieving what we truly desire. For example, let's imagine that you really want to find a life partner, but you constantly tell yourself: "I'll never meet someone" or "All the good ones are taken." If your message to yourself is that you won't find a partner, that's the outcome you will create for yourself. Or if you want to be a professional stage performer, but you subconsciously repeat to yourself the message, handed down from your parents, that you're not good enough, you'll end up manifesting that negative message. It becomes a self-fulfilling prophecy. What we tell ourselves plays out.

Even when we know the importance of maintaining positive messaging and self-talk, we can still sometimes slip into negativity. After all, we're human. But if we remain committed to the idea and vigilant about catching ourselves, we can immediately reframe our words into positive language.

Exchanging negative words for positive ones isn't about being uptight or a superficial Pollyanna. It's a way of taking ownership of our experience by affirming what we *do* want. Since we're programming our reality with our words, we may as well use words that reinforce how we want things to unfold. If your desired outcome feels like too much of a stretch, don't worry about it. Just think of it as if you're practicing your lines, "rehearsing" for your new reality.

The same idea applies to how we envision details our future unfolding. Science has established a strong connection between mind and body, thoughts and outcomes. This connection is the essence behind the practice of visualization. Professional athletes often mentally rehearse outcomes. The neural pathways they create through their imaginations pave the way for physical results. Think about it: Every physical action starts in your brain. So the more you practice seeing the outcomes you desire in your mind's eye, the more you'll reinforce the connection, and the more likely you'll be to achieve your goals.

If you want a job at your dream company, imagine yourself crushing it in your interview. If you want to grow your business, imagine just the right clients and partners showing up in your life. Why not also imagine it happening with minimal effort on your part? If you want to score a goal in your upcoming soccer game, visualize how you'll position yourself to take the perfect shot. If you're scheduled to give a presentation, picture yourself at the podium sharing your knowledge with a captivated audience. Every time we take ownership of our lives by thinking encouraging words and imagining the outcomes we desire, we help them become true. Verbalizing and visualizing the future as we'd like it to unfold is a way of inviting it in.

LESSON 9:
SELF-ADVOCACY

To honor the self is to be willing to think independently, to live by our own mind, and to have the courage of our own perceptions and judgments. To honor the self is to be willing to know not only what we think but also what we feel, what we want, need, desire, suffer over, are frightened or angered by—and to accept our right to experience such feelings.

–Joan Borysenko[15]

Honoring oneself can seem like a luxury. In our overworked culture where being constantly busy is often mistaken for success, it can be a real challenge to take

---

15   Joan Borysenko, *Guilt Is the Teacher, Love Is the Lesson* (Warner Books, 1991), p. 46.

time out to nurture the self. This is especially true for women, as many of us are conditioned to put others' needs first, tending to everyone except ourselves. However, when our own needs are met, we're in a much better position to give to others. We are more likely to respond to situations generously, with love, creativity, and a level head, when we practice self-advocacy.

Growing up, many of us were told not to be selfish and taught to be people pleasers. Our parents may have even modeled that behavior. I used to be afraid that if I stated my needs, I might inconvenience someone. I was also afraid of being perceived as pushy or controlling. I figured it was my job to accommodate others. For some reason, it was important to me to come across as easygoing, flexible, and "low maintenance." I took *pride* in being that way—able to set my needs aside for others. To me, it was a sign of fortitude.

The problem was that I had grown so accustomed to placing others' needs above mine that I came to believe I didn't have preferences at all. When making decisions with a group of people, whether at work or socially, I would avoid taking a strong position. It wasn't that I didn't have preferences; I just wasn't factoring them into the equation. Deep down, I believed that my needs didn't matter—not exactly the same thing as being low-maintenance.

Thoughts like these make it very challenging to be assertive. How can we possibly ask for what we want if we don't *know* what we want? If we don't self-advocate, we risk feeling anger and resentment toward others.

We feel small and insignificant. This feeds our sense of unworthiness, and it becomes a vicious cycle. This is why it's so important to take responsibility by being honest and forthright in expressing our truth.

I spend a lot of time with my clients teaching them to program into their daily modus operandi a step where they stop to take a breath and consider what they want. As they practice considering their needs and then verbalizing them, they quickly realize that self-advocacy isn't about being selfish, inconsiderate, or demanding.

When we ask for what we need, people appreciate our directness. Knowing clearly what we want makes it simpler and easier on **them**. When we hem and haw, they have to wait and wonder how to help. On the other hand, when we frame our wishes clearly and directly, people know exactly what to do. They can say yes or no, depending on whether they are willing and able to accommodate us. And everyone can sidestep all the back-and-forth that results from misunderstandings created by vague communication.

Negotiating Self-Advocacy

Advocating for ourselves isn't a complicated concept, but it makes a profound difference in our daily lives. Once we make it a regular practice to ask for what we want, we no longer harbor second thoughts about speaking up. We stop suppressing our feelings. If our latte isn't made the way we like, we politely ask for a fix. If we are freezing in a restaurant, we kindly ask if it is possible to turn down the air. Typically such requests, when issued respectfully and without entitlement, are well received. The person making your coffee or serving your meal wants you to be happy—not suffering in silence.

When we create a new habit of asking for what we want, oftentimes we expose the fallacy of our prior beliefs. We can put an end to the chronic—and unnecessary—feelings of disappointment, discomfort, and stress that we otherwise create when we withhold. We stop being martyrs. We expand out of our comfort zones.

Imagine that your boss asks you to take on a project that's appealing to you, but you're afraid you won't be able to complete it successfully without additional resources. You might assume that your company wouldn't give them to you, and possibly be afraid of how it would make you look if you asked. Instead, you try to do the whole project on your own. You even put in extra hours of your personal time. Before you know it, what you thought would be a fun and rewarding project instead becomes stressful and begins to compromise your other work.

What if someone on your team could have shared the load—someone with the expertise, extra bandwidth, and enthusiasm for the project? And what if all it would have taken to get that person's help was expressing your concerns from the very beginning?

We should never assume that advocating for ourselves, or asking for what we need, will make us a nuisance to others. And we never know what opportunities we might be denying ourselves and others when we don't state our needs. We can honor our own needs without compromising others'. Though it may be hard to believe, the two aren't necessarily in conflict. In fact, oftentimes there's no conflict at all, because you're the *only* one who has a preference.

Consider this example. You and your friends are planning to go out for dinner. One friend suggests a restaurant, but you have a hankering for your favorite meal at a different place. You might agree to her suggestion to avoid being difficult, but deep down, you'd feel disappointed. Now imagine that maybe your friend just wanted to be helpful by making a quick decision that would simplify the planning for everyone. And maybe she didn't really care where or what she ate. Wouldn't it be a waste of energy to have withheld your preferences?

Some of my best applications of self-advocacy have been in my marriage. In the past, I would become frustrated if Marc forgot to do a chore. Over time, as the chore remained incomplete, I would grow resentful. I'd stew about it, contemplating how I might broach a reminder. Fearing that my words and tone would betray my true feeling, I would become paralyzed over *how* to say what I wanted. I would say nothing and instead brood, which Marc no doubt picked up on. The new, more skilled Ali began to simply and plainly tell him what I wanted. There was no longer anything to hide—neither my needs nor my secret negative feelings. He noticed the change in me and appreciated it.

When we're clear and direct, we can ask for what we want without any subtext of hidden emotion. Our words will come across at face value.

Self-Care and Self-Optimization

If speaking up for ourselves is an outer manifestation of self-advocacy, self-care is our inner manifestation. We know that problems often spring up at the worst moments. Kids, for example, seem to demand our attention most urgently when we're already running late, in the middle of cooking dinner, or, worse, at the airport as we're making our way through the security line. These are times when our patience is in short supply. When our resources are taxed, it's enormously difficult to create space to respond as our best selves.

The ideas of ownership and choice that we discussed in the previous lesson apply directly to our ability to foster healthy responses and avoid negative reactions. Taking responsibility for our personal care is how we mitigate the effects of poor timing and unfavorable context.

By nurturing our well-being on the physical, mental, emotional, and spiritual levels, we shore up our energy stores. When crises fall upon us, we have the reserves to maintain presence of mind and heart. We don't get swept up in fight-or-flight and react impulsively. Instead, we *respond.* We make conscious decisions that are aligned with what we want. The best versions of ourselves come forward as we show up for others with our full attention. On the outside this looks like what we call "patience." But really, it's love.

When we replenish ourselves on a consistent basis, the implicit message we send to ourselves is that we matter. Self-advocacy is about doing right for ourselves. When we take the time to do this, we are not being selfish. We're in fact increasing our ability to give. We honor ourselves and others when we take care of ourselves and state our needs and desires honestly and courageously. Instead of having superficial relationships where we don't show ourselves and don't state our preferences, we live openly and deepen our connection with others.

I let go of all responsibility except the responsibility—and the satisfaction—of being myself. For me it was a most unusual feeling: to be comfortably irresponsible with no feelings of guilt. And, to my surprise, I found I was more effective that way.

–Carl Rogers[16]

---

[16]   Carl Rogers, *A Way of Being* (Mariner Books, 1995), p. 81.

LESSON 10:
ACCEPTANCE

If you'd like a prescription for a Grace-filled life, resolve here and now to refrain from judging anyone or anything, most of all yourself, from this day forward.

–H. Ronald Hulnick and Mary R. Hulnick[17]

The concept of **acceptance** is a beautiful gift in our lives. It can profoundly affect our sense of inner peace and well-being. Acceptance entails only a small tweak in mindset. With that shift, we gain control over how we feel in the wake of the otherwise exasperating events of day-to-day life.

---

[17] H. Ronald Hulnick and Mary R. Hulnick, *Loyalty to Your Soul* (Hay House, 2010), p. 159.

Acceptance requires an understanding that all people are doing the best they can at any given time. We might *believe* that a person is capable of more. We might **want** them to do better. But the reality is that if they could do better, they would. We have no choice but to accept what they've offered us in that moment.

Viewing people and events through this lens frees us of judgments, both negative and positive. Though it may sound counterintuitive, even positive judgments have a downside. They can create a confirmation bias[18] that may lead us astray. For example, when we put someone on a pedestal, we may overvalue their opinions and base our decisions on *their* beliefs rather than doing what is best for us. When we don't objectively evaluate what we hear, we may even get duped, intentionally or unintentionally. This can happen, in particular, in the presence of charismatic or influential people.

When we're in a mindset of acceptance, all we see is what *is*. As Shakespeare wrote in *Hamlet*, "[T]here is nothing either good or bad, but thinking makes it so." When we're able to observe with neutrality, without judging people's thoughts or actions as good or bad, we experience greater equanimity and peace of mind. We let go of emotional charge and inaccurate biases that can trip us up.

---

[18] "Confirmation bias" was coined in 1960 by English psychologist Peter Wason and is defined as "the tendency to interpret new evidence as confirmation of one's existing beliefs or theories." (https://www.dictionary.com/browse/confirmation-bias?s=t).

I used to feel so distracted, at times, by my judgments that I would struggle to speak up. I worried that my attitude would show through and that I'd sound impolite or angry. When I learned to set my judgments aside, I became more free. It became much easier to authentically communicate whatever was on my mind.

An acceptance mindset allows us to become more open-minded about the way events play out. It helps us let go of expectations that often lead to anger and disappointment. A judgmental frame of mind distinguishes everything along the lines of good/bad and right/wrong. This kind of thinking limits our options. It makes it hard for us to recognize the difference between people's impact and intentions. Rigid beliefs create restriction, leaving us ill at ease and making it harder for us to connect with qualities of love, kindness, and compassion.

Say you enter into a partnership—whether personal or professional—and expect a 50/50 split across all roles. It doesn't quite work out the way you assumed it would, and the relationships sours. But if you could free yourself from judgments, you would put yourself in a better position to hear guidance from your small, wise inner voice. Did you really want a 50/50 split to begin with? Perhaps you always envisioned a leadership role. Maybe you even knew going into the partnership that the division wouldn't be equal. As your ideas of right and wrong fade away, you might connect with your deeper needs. You might discover that a 50/50 split isn't the best route. Perhaps you'd be better off creating a division of labor that honors your individual strengths and interests.

When we accept what is, we can slow down, take a breath, and reflect on our situation with greater clarity and objectivity. It's worth noting that slowing down to give ourselves the space to observe and reflect does not slow down our outer results. When we remove the distraction that comes from a whirlwind of judgmental thoughts, answers usually come more quickly and clearly, and they tend to be higher quality, which ends up saving us time and energy.

When we are in a state of acceptance, we meet people where they are. Say you have a sibling who drives you crazy—who always runs late or is disorganized or seems thoughtless. Instead of judging your sibling, imagine holding space for them and loving them fully as they are—shortcomings and all. As Carl Rogers explains in *A Way of Being*, "To care for this person for what he or she is, dropping my own expectations of what I want him or her to be for me, dropping my desire to change this person to suit my needs, is a most difficult but enriching way to a satisfying intimate relationship."[19]

Once we stop foisting our expectations on others, we allow for genuine appreciation. Accepting someone, even if their actions have hurt you, is not about being a doormat or disrespecting yourself. More than anything, it's a way of recognizing that someone else's actions are not about **you**; they're about **them**. They have weaknesses, challenges, and fears of their own. We can actually shift to an attitude of compassion—which can be a further reminder not to take their actions personally. This can

---

[19] Carl Rogers, *A Way of Being* (Mariner Books, 1995), p. 85.

help us relax and make room for their strengths to come forward, as well as our own.

I've known parents of children with behavioral issues or special needs who simply cannot accept their children's challenges. They want their children to be a certain way. Even when teachers, grandparents, or trusted friends raise their awareness of problems that are obvious, they are not able to recognize them. Rather than acknowledging the reality of their children's needs, they insist that there isn't an issue, often bending over backward and blaming outside parties.

When we drop our expectations for how we **want** others to be, we can accept and love them as they **are**. Where there are problems, our acceptance allows us to put our energy toward finding solutions and building bridges.

One area where many of us can practice acceptance is the aging process. In Western culture, we attempt to thwart aging rather than celebrating it. We view the body's changes in negative terms, frowning at wrinkles and gray hair and age spots. Part of this is natural. We fear death, and watching loved ones age can be painful. There's a reason acceptance is the fifth and final stage of the grief cycle. But as soon as we learn to accept what is, we come back to our hearts, where we find peace.

A client of mine once shared with me how much she was struggling with the reality of her parents' aging. She had always viewed them as active and vibrant and had admired them for these qualities. She saw them often and turned to them for both friendship and counsel. But lately she had been finding that she wasn't agreeing so much with their points of view anymore. Their counsel no longer felt relevant and applicable; they were in a different stage of life. She was saddened to see them slowing down. Consequently, she was struggling with feelings of anger and frustration, even loss. As she did her inner work, she began to come into a state of acceptance. She realized she needed to accept where her parents were rather than longing for where she wished they could be. All of this paved the way for her to build a new relationship with them—still based in love, but reflective of the current state of affairs.

Another example we can all relate to is when we get sick or injured. It can be so difficult on many levels. On top of the discomfort of not feeling great, we also have to deal with disappointment, stress, and possibly even embarrassment. Maybe there's an event we've been looking forward to that we'll have to miss. Or maybe it's a particularly busy time at work and we're already feeling a lot of pressure—these are the times we usually do get sick—and now we're afraid we'll fall even further behind. Plus, not being able to do our jobs fully or having to rely on others for help can be very difficult to accept. But the sooner we can stop resisting the reality of sickness and start showing ourselves some tenderness, the sooner we recover.

There are so many areas of life where acceptance can mean the difference between aggravation and inner peace or enthusiasm. When we are able to accept the difficult parts of a process, we can feel lightness and flow along the way.

Finding our way to acceptance can be a tall order. Sometimes, even when we are aware that there's an opportunity to experience it, we just can't seem to detect the path. But it can be helpful just to have the knowledge that acceptance is where our answer ultimately lies.

Let's look at some examples of how a state of full acceptance might sound:

- *I accept that what will be, will be. Where I feel sad or challenged, there are important lessons to be learned. The challenges I face are here, ultimately, for my own benefit. They are gifts in disguise, even if I cannot see them that way in this moment. There is a reason I'm not being given the experience I want.*

- *There will be painful and discouraging moments, but I trust that something valuable and meaningful lies ahead, beyond my ego's judgments and desires.*

- *I accept that what I'm going through will take as much time as it requires. It may not conform to my timeline. If I am open to the experience, I will receive benefits that surpass anything I could have envisioned on my own. For that reason, I am open to the lessons available to me in having to surrender to a timeline and state of affairs that don't correspond with my wishes.*

- *I accept that I may not know what is best for me in my life's journey. I trust that whatever comes from this process will be for the highest good.*

- *I accept whatever life brings—even if I don't like it—and I am committed to being present, joyful, and filled with gratitude for the life I've been given.*

When we are on a path to mastery in any area of life, we will be presented with increasingly difficult challenges. This is a good sign that we are learning and making progress with our soul's lessons. As we go along, we need to keep reminding ourselves that, in order to create our ideal experiences or circumstances, we must start with the reality of **what is**. Otherwise, our hopes are just fantasies based on circumstances that aren't true. The longer we resist what is, the more pain we'll feel. When we move into acceptance, we can embrace our feelings and our challenges and look for opportunities to love and to learn important life lessons. We can expand our feelings of inner peace and joy.

LESSON 11:
SELF-FORGIVENESS

Forgiveness is not an occasional act,
it is a constant attitude.

–Martin Luther King Jr.

Everything we discussed on the topic of acceptance applies as much to how we relate to ourselves as it does to how we relate to others. An important way we can cultivate acceptance—of ourselves or of others—is through forgiveness.

We all know the word "forgiveness," but how well do we understand what it means? How do we navigate our way into a state of true forgiveness when needed? Most of my life, my understanding of the concept was shallow at best.

Memory isn't perfect, but if I'm not mistaken, it's possible that for most of my adult life, I had never forgiven anyone for anything. I chalked it up to my perfectionist tendencies: I surrounded myself with amazing people who never made mistakes in the first place. If someone did do something I objected to, I would conclude that they weren't the person I'd imagined. I'd feel disappointed, lose interest in them as a friend, and that would be the end. I wouldn't even look back. I'd just move on, without even having a conversation about it. This felt right to me. People either met my standards or they didn't.

In hindsight, it sounds so harsh. But back then, I didn't understand how forgiveness could be applied to others. The idea that it could be applied to *ourselves* had never even crossed my mind. Obviously, we can't control what others do, but it seemed to me we should be able to meet our own expectations—if something is important enough to us. If we try hard enough, we shouldn't ever have to fall short. Therefore, there'd be no occasion for forgiveness to come into play. But it turns out that the willingness and ability to forgive is an essential skill if we want to cultivate maximum well-being *and* achieve our goals.

We now know that, as humans, we are fallible—no matter how smart, talented, or dedicated we are. As we've discussed throughout this book (think back to the lessons on Spirit, ego, humility, acceptance), we have limitations. We can't do everything, and we all have things we're just not very good at. We can't always live up to our standards. At times like this, forgiveness can be like a magic elixir. It brings an incredible sense of relief. And there aren't any downsides.

So, what does forgiveness look like from an evolved point of view? It's not about letting ourselves or someone else off the hook undeservedly. Rather, it's about remembering that we're all human and cutting ourselves some slack. It's about showing ourselves love and compassion, even when we make missteps. It's about letting go of our judgments.

For example, instead of calling ourselves names—stupid, fat, ugly, lazy—we can proactively put an end to our insults. Remember, this is all just part of the ego's chatter, the loop of thoughts in our minds. Our words stick. The more we speak like this to ourselves, the more we actually believe these messages to be true. So rather than beating ourselves up mercilessly or focusing on every flaw, we replace our message of criticism with tenderness and empathy. We offer comfort and understanding to ourselves. We forgive ourselves.

Think of it this way: If a friend or loved one were struggling, would you kick him when he's down? Typically, we are far more critical of ourselves than we are of others, but if we wouldn't be unkind to people we care about, why do we do it to ourselves? It's not only hurtful but also unproductive.

Every time we catch ourselves being unkind, we can shift our focus from judgment and criticism to self-forgiveness. We call this practice **compassionate self-forgiveness**. It allows us to move beyond our shortcomings and mistakes so we can better claim our power.

I'll give an example of a time it really worked wonders for me. One day, I decided to take a walk with Cooper to our local amusement park at the Santa Monica Pier. I didn't realize that I was setting myself up for a miserable adventure.

Internally, I was contending with my own sensitivities: I felt overwhelmed by the loud, chaotic environment, I felt germophobic at the thought of all the sticky hands that had touched every surface, and every time I dropped more coins into the arcade games, I chastised myself for wasting money.

Meanwhile, Cooper was darting from one game to another while I frantically tried to keep up, wrestling his empty stroller through the tight, crowded space, trying not to lose sight of him. He wanted to play every game but of course didn't have the attention span to wait for me to read the instructions and teach him. Neither did I, frankly. It wasn't long before he crumpled onto the ground in a full-blown—and very loud—tantrum.

In the past, I would have immediately felt like a terrible mother. Instead, this time, I realized that I could forgive myself. I acknowledged that I didn't like the situation I had created but recognized that I was doing the best I could. I reminded myself that, even though I may not have had the knowledge and awareness to pick a different activity, one bad day didn't make me a bad mother in the grand scheme of things. This way of being was entirely novel to me—I can't emphasize enough what a relief it was. Plus, I was able to shift my attention and focus away from *myself* and beating myself up, and instead concentrate on supporting **him** through his big emotions.

Our negative thoughts need not take up space in our consciousness. They're not uplifting, beneficial, or useful. They only get in the way of our becoming who we want to be. When we stop focusing on our flaws, we free ourselves to show up in the world as we wish to see ourselves.

Compassionate self-forgiveness also has long-term benefits. Each time a negative judgment creeps into our minds, if we stop right away and forgive ourselves, we can avoid perpetuating the negative beliefs and thought patterns that prevent us from being our best selves.

After a little practice with promptly forgiving ourselves for judgments, we get better at it. Eventually, many of our judgments will stop showing up at all. A consistent practice of self-forgiveness sends a powerful message to our judgments that they are not welcome. Self-forgiveness is like standing up to a bully.

Never forget that to forgive yourself is to release trapped energy that could be doing good work in the world.

–D. Patrick Miller[20]

---

[20] D. Patrick Miller, *The Forgiveness Book: Healing the Hurts We Don't Deserve* (Hampton Roads, 2017), p. 41.

LESSON 12:
INTENTIONS

The moment one definitely commits oneself, then Providence moves too. All sorts of things occur to help one that would never otherwise have occurred… unforeseen incidents and meetings and material assistance, which no man could have dreamt would have come his way.

—William Hutchison Murray[21]

Setting intentions is one of the more straightforward lessons. It is particularly well suited for those of us who are achievement driven.

---

21 William Hutchison Murray, *The Scottish Himalayan Expedition* (Dent, 1951), p.7.

We all know what intentions are. We commonly think of them as the underlying desire, purpose, or rationale behind our actions. At times, we associate them with something positive, as in "good intentions." Spiritually speaking, setting intentions is a way of aligning our consciousness with a hope or goal. It serves to unite our mind, body, and spirit in a way that helps bring about desired outcomes.

Prior to studying spirituality, I rarely set intentions for myself. It had never occurred to me to try. But once I began to incorporate the practice into my daily life, it came as quite a revelation that something so easy could be such a powerful tool in my tool kit.

The very first time I consciously decided to take a moment to think about my intention for a future experience, I was amazed by the results. I felt like I had experienced magic. I was about to begin one of my first sessions as a coach, and I started to feel nervous about how I would do. I really wanted to bring my "A game" and provide value to my client. As my fears began their monologue of what-ifs—what if I'm not good enough, insightful enough, wise enough, perceptive enough—I changed the channel of my thoughts and instead tuned in to an intention for what I **wanted**. I set my intention to let go of any demands on myself to think or say the right things and instead to just be present with my client and listen with my full heart.

The session went great. My client gained new awareness about herself, let go of limiting beliefs that were no longer serving her, and found her way to a feeling of peace and acceptance around the situation she was facing. As for me, I felt the kind of connection I live for—connection with the person in front of me, with Spirit, and with my own gifts and capacity to be of service. The simple act of focusing on what I wanted had set in motion everything necessary to make it happen.

Over time, in working with many clients, I noticed how beneficial and empowering it was for people in all different types of situations to set intentions. When we shift our attention away from our worries and confusion and toward the outcome we desire or the feeling we wish to experience, we free ourselves of unnecessary stress and invite in possibility.

In my own life, I've set intentions in all kinds of situations. I've employed them to help me deliver bad news or spend time with people who have challenging personalities. I've stated them to myself before family get-togethers to help smooth out any potential difficulties. When I've had a particularly busy day ahead of me, I've set intentions beforehand to define my goals. I've also used them as a tool to help me perform in higher-stakes situations such as interviews and presentations for work.

One important point to consider when setting intentions is that, while the exercise is about bringing into focus the outcome we desire, we must **let go** of any expectation or attachment to that outcome. The reason is twofold. First, if we hold on too tight, we could block the outcome by trying too hard to control **how** it happens. Second, our desired outcomes may show up in disguise. Sometimes what we need doesn't manifest the way we expect. In fact, it may look like the opposite of what we want. We need to remain open so we are able to recognize it and see how it's exactly what we needed.

Getting results…depends on clarity and commitment. You'll need to commit to your dream, really wanting it to come true. But you can't commit to your dream unless you know what it is. You do that by finding your true heart's desire. It will speak through your creative conscience in a few simple words.

–Lucia Capacchione[22]

---

22   Lucia Capacchione, *Visioning* (Jeremy P. Tarcher/Putnam, 2000), p. 58.

LESSON 13:
MIND-BODY PARTNERSHIP

─◆◆◆─

*You can begin the fulfillment of this intention to
live a life of self-respect by honoring the temple that
houses you. You know what to do. You don't need
another diet, workout manual, or personal trainer.
Go within, listen to your body, and treat it with all
the dignity and love that your self-respect demands.*

—Wayne Dyer[23]

─◆◆◆─

Most of us live between our ears. We walk around thinking incessantly about what we need to do, replaying
past events, anticipating the future. The wheels don't
stop turning. Personally, from the earliest time I can

---

[23]   Wayne Dyer, *The Power of Intention* (Hay House, 2010), p. 15.

remember, I revered the power of the mind. I believed in the **strength** of my mind to come up with a solution to any problem.

Even with physical issues, I believed I could beat my body into submission through wishful thinking. I saw myself as being able to transcend the physical–as though my body were something that could be conquered. If I began feeling under the weather, I would refuse to submit and instead keep pushing through toward my goals. If I later reached a point where I could no longer deny the inevitability of becoming sick, I would cave in–but I would give myself a deadline to recover. I'd allow myself one day to stay home and sleep it off, insisting that I'd be back in action the following day.

The same was true for how I handled pain; I would ignore my body's needs. When my back pain first became noticeable, I thought I had too much work to do to stop and address the issue. I believed that through mind over matter, I could make the pain disappear. To me, the pain was some kind of nuisance. I would curse and berate it. It was as though my body were a separate entity that existed merely to serve my cognitive needs.

I never showed my body the kind of respect that would have acknowledged its true role as a partner to my mind in the broader scheme of my life and my pursuits. Not surprisingly, the more I ignored my pain, the worse it got. And the worse it got, the more embittered I became.

The body is our friend. It is on our side. If the body could express one desire, it would be to work with us.

The body certainly doesn't want to cause trouble. But remember, the only way a body can communicate is through sensations—pleasure and pain. When something isn't right, the body tries to get our attention through subtle messages. Maybe a small headache or a twinge. The question is whether we're listening—and how we respond.

If we consistently ignore its early signals, the body will have no choice but to amplify its statement in progressively louder and more forceful ways—until we acknowledge that we've received its message. When we don't heed the body's signals, we curtail its ability to be a supportive partner to us in the things we want to do.

If we want to accomplish our goals, we need to treat the body not as a subordinate but as an equal and valued member of the team. We should give our bodies the respect they deserve by listening. By responding early to their quiet and subtle signs, taking care of issues while they're small, we can reduce the likelihood that our bodies will have to scream at us later on. When we treat our bodies with kindness, they will do the same and take care of "us." With this understanding, we can commit to a new agreement of partnership, respect, and mutual support.

The good news is that just because our bodies can't express themselves in words doesn't mean we can't dialogue with them. Through a technique known in psychology as "Gestalt," we can address questions directly to our bodies. Traditionally, a therapist might invite a client to have a dialogue with the part of him- or herself that's causing distress, but we can easily replicate the premise outside the therapeutic setting.

All you need to do is ask your body a question, then sit in silence as you listen for the answer. You might ask something as simple as "What specifically is my knee pain trying to communicate?" Obviously, your body won't speak out loud, but its answer may come to you in the form of a thought. And when it does, it will feel like a self-evident truth.

The idea that your body has its own mind and voice may seem hokey, but if you can get past that, you will be on your way to establishing a healthy partnership with this part of you that you must rely on to exist in the world.

The Gestalt process has proved transformative for so many people. In my own life, dialoguing with my back pain taught me an eye-opening lesson, and I felt like I had made a new yet lifelong friend. I now truly recognize that we are one and the same. I no longer ignore pain. I understand at a deep level that doing so will just slow me down, making it harder to engage in my goals and pursuits.

This system can also serve us well with more common-place and transient pain. For example, if you develop a headache during a meeting, you might take a moment to address it directly: "Why are you here? Why now?" Perhaps you'll realize that you've been dreading this meeting without having been consciously aware of it. Maybe you've been experiencing subtle tension with a coworker, and the problems are beginning to come to a head. It's worth considering that, oftentimes, something as simple as a headache can be the body's way of speaking up. I remember a time when I didn't appreciate the way a colleague was treating me, and I began to experience reflux symptoms. My colleague's behavior had become "indigestible." It was getting to the point that I could longer "stomach" it. These figurative ways of expressing our feelings can have literal roots.

The body draws us into the present. By listening to it and acknowledging it, we receive real-time feedback. We can't be expected to perform at our peak for extended periods without replenishing ourselves. Sometimes slowing down to protect our bodies isn't a sign of laziness or lack of dedication but rather what's necessary. When we do so, we often find just what we need to move forward and be on our way.

The simple act of inquiring and then listening to the body is powerful. It is truly a worthwhile exercise. There is, however, one important caveat. Sometimes having conversations with our bodies will force us to confront issues that have been under the radar. Perhaps, in the case of the meeting headache, you will realize an uncomfortable truth you don't want to see. Maybe you realize you need to have a difficult conversation or make a change. The body ushers in insights. And while they are not always welcome, they will help us grow.

As we pay closer attention to our bodies, we begin to notice our tendencies and how we are proceeding. In whatever we're doing, our goal should be to work not harder but rather smarter, more effortlessly, and more joyfully. We want to be on the path of least resistance—in all our endeavors.

In closing, I want to mention that the messages we send our bodies are as important as the ones we receive. A tool that can help assist us during challenging times is a focus image. I often work with clients to help them find a calming or inspiring image to anchor them and bring them into their bodies during times of stress. For myself, I once chose the focus image of a tree: a beautiful oak, just about the perfect size for climbing, with thick branches and full leaves. Majestic and regal, this image would help ground and center me. It projected the idea of strength and picturing it would help remind me of my strong inner core and ability to harness my flexibility to meet the elements around me.

I shared this image with a friend, who tried to use the same one. It didn't work for her. She found the tree *too* grounded. She realized she often felt in her personal life as though she were stuck in the mud. She ended up turning to a dance image. It felt freer and more uplifting. When she focused on the image of a dancer, she felt powerful and sublime.

Take a moment to think of a focus image that might be helpful to you. It should be personal to you and feel relevant to the phase of life you're in. During times of stress, take a moment to concentrate on your image. Allow its message to sink into your thoughts. Perhaps it will help you reestablish the connection between your mind and body. Welcome this insight. Your focus image may change over time as you evolve. No matter what, it should help you feel more appreciation and gratitude for your body and all it does for you.

LESSON 14:

THE MYTH OF "WORK-LIFE BALANCE"

*I believe happiness and joy are the purpose of life.
If we know that the future will be very dark or
painful, then we lose our determination to live.
Therefore, life is something based on hope.... An
innate quality among sentient beings, particularly
among human beings, is the urge or strong feeling
to encounter or experience happiness and discard
suffering or pain. Therefore, the whole basis of
human life is the experience of different levels of
happiness. Achieving or experiencing happiness is the
purpose of life.*

–His Holiness the Dalai Lama[24]

---

24 Quoted in Carol Adrienne, *The Purpose of Your Life* (New York: Eagle Brook, 1998), p. 69.

Many of my clients first come to me seeking career advice. They feel stuck or unfulfilled or burnt out, just as I once did in my job. Some of them express a desire for "work-life balance." Moments like these always makes me smile. The person typically sounds so eager, hopeful that I can give them an answer (perhaps an article or a book) that will crack the code safeguarding that mystical solution.

After many years of working with clients, listening to the stories of friends and colleagues, and thinking about my own journey in depth, I've concluded that there's no such thing. It's a myth. So many of us are chasing an illusion. So if you feel overwhelmed by the goal of trying to find balance, go ahead and strike it off your list entirely.

When we think about what we need to do to take care of ourselves holistically, the work-life-balance paradigm is not very useful to us anyway. In this lesson we'll look at how and why that model is flawed, and I'll introduce you to a new model. Why have we focused so much attention on work-life balance in the first place? I think it's because we've mistakenly conceived of it as an end, when in fact it's a means. The jewel we've really been after all this time is **happiness**.

The good news is that, unlike the events and duties of our work and personal lives, achieving happiness is within our control. No matter our circumstances—as we've learned—we can always find ways to reframe our experiences and use them to help us learn, grow, and appreciate our lives and all that we have. We can apply all the skills we've learned in this book to nudge us toward happiness.

So, let's define happiness. At the macro level, happiness typically comes from having a sense of purpose. This is achieved by working toward something personally meaningful that is interesting to us, that we're good at, and that we value. When we know who we are and that what we're doing matters, we feel content. In my life, I am happiest when I feel connected to the people around me in some way and to my highest self. At times like this, I perceive myself as being at my peak, bringing forward my best qualities in service to myself and others.

At the micro level, or how you feel in a given moment, happiness comes from the feeling of being centered, whole, and fully present. If you were in the midst of working on a project, happiness might look like this: Inspiration would be abundant and you'd be in a flow. There'd be no feeling of stress or struggle. Concentration would be effortless. You'd be focused, with crystal-clear thoughts and ideas. If someone were to interrupt you in the moment and ask how you were doing, you would reflect on the question and respond sincerely with an enthusiastic "Great!"

Happiness can range in duration and intensity. Sometimes it's only momentary, showing up intermittently in brief flashes. Other times it can endure over a period of days, weeks, or months.

When we talk about happiness, the word "success" inevitably comes up. As discussed at the start of this book, we often think success will produce happiness. But it's actually the other way around. When you're happy and doing what you love, you will be successful. In fact, you already are. As far as I'm concerned, **doing what you love** *is* **success**—because by definition it brings happiness.

When we're fully present and engaged, working with a clear mind and a full and peaceful heart, we not only enjoy what we are doing but also do a better job. It's similar to the idea of abundance—the happiness we feel is an important indicator of success, and this uplifted state breeds more happiness and success. It's a virtuous cycle. There's no final destination we need to reach, because we feel good about ourselves all along the way. We might as well stay in the delightful present.

This is why success shouldn't be narrowly defined. It isn't just what we accomplish on our list of achievements. Success is how we feel on the inside as we work toward our goals. It's the experience of inner peace, a clear mind, and an open heart. It's a certain lightness of being as we engage with all aspects of our lives. For myself, I recognize success as the feeling that I'm being the best version of myself for a sustained period of time.

This fuller definition of success takes into account how others feel in our presence. Are we being kind and thoughtful toward others? Can people readily see and feel our good intentions? Do people feel emotionally safe and seen in our presence? In their interactions with us, do they feel appreciated for who they are? If you can answer yes to these questions, then you are successful.

And being able to show up in the world in these ways is probably as much a result of being happy as it is a driver that's generating your feeling of happiness.

Flaws in the Work-Life-Balance Paradigm

The entire work-life-balance paradigm is flawed. What does the concept even mean? Does it mean having just the right amounts of "work" and "life"? Or is it about having separation between the two? The conundrum is that oftentimes we cannot control how much of each is thrown at us. Nor we can effectively separate them.

The idea of "balance" is also misguided. Even if you were to strike a magical equilibrium, it would be short-lived. Balance is a static state, and work and life are anything but. Our busy lives keep us moving, shifting, and adapting to new circumstances all the time. In other words, any moments of equilibrium while teetering on the tightrope are fleeting. Something will inevitably come along and throw you off balance again. The very nature of life constantly causes us to wobble. That it's challenging to remain balanced doesn't signal a failing on our part. There's nothing about it that needs to be fixed or changed. It's the process of life.

So, if happiness is the gold we're really after, the map we draw must show us the way to nurturing our mind, body, and soul. This is the most effective path to maximizing our physical and mental energy. After all, this is the key to living our best life from day to day.

Holistic Happiness and Our Four Flowerpots

Our mind, body, and soul are our component parts. If we want true success, we need to focus on all aspects of our humanity. We do that by taking care of our needs on four levels: **physical**, **mental**, **emotional**, and **spiritual**.

All the concepts, tools, and practices in this book are about nurturing ourselves accordingly. The lessons are all focused on these levels in different ways. When we combine all of our lessons, when we engage with them, we bring the mind, body, and soul into harmony.

The rewards of following the regime are vast. Yet when we get unusually busy or narrowly focused on just one area of life, it can be easy to "fall off the wagon." This, of course, is when we most need to engage with our lessons. There's no denying that nurturing ourselves is an ongoing, lifelong commitment that takes discipline and constant course corrections—informed by our inner GPS—along the way.

To nurture ourselves, we might imagine four flowerpots, representing our physical, mental, emotional, and spiritual levels. Each pot is carefully chosen and prepared with nutritious potting soil and the seeds of our favorite flowers. It's our job to water each one on a regular basis to help our seeds sprout and bloom.

When you commit to watering all four flowerpots, you'll discover that it's irrelevant whether your personal and professional lives are balanced. What you'll notice is that you are tending to yourself. You will feel centered and present. You will also feel more energetic. This will pay dividends across all areas of your life.

PHYSICAL	Everything having to do with • our bodies • our environment • tangible things such as goals, accomplishments, and finances
MENTAL	Everything having to do with using our minds: • strategic thinking, planning, and decision making • creative and intellectual pursuits • activities that keep us challenged, motivated, engaged
EMOTIONAL	Everything to do with our feelings, including • sense of self-worth • how we experience, recognize, and express our feelings • relationships with colleagues, family, and friends
SPIRITUAL	Our feeling of connection with the larger world: • sense of meaning and purpose • beliefs, values, and ethics • love, wisdom, beauty, inspiration

It's worth noting that our personal and professional lives aren't that different in the big picture. It's a false dichotomy, as there's actually a lot of overlap between the two. This is why when we love the work we do, it may not feel like work at all. Likewise, some of the things we have to do out of necessity in our personal lives may feel very much like work—for example, cleaning the bathroom. Our personal and professional lives both have the potential to contribute to as well as detract from our physical, mental, emotional, and spiritual well-being. It's easier to see this when, instead of thinking of work and life as separate, we look at our lives according to the four areas of our human **being**. The chart above represents a more integrated way of thinking about both challenges and goals, as well as the parts of life that bring us joy.

To nurture our well-being, we must consider not just the things we need to get done in our lives but also the things in each area that we **want** to do—the things we **love** doing because **they feel good to us**. These things are the water we pour into our flowerpots to help us feel nurtured.

In the exercise related to this lesson, I'll show you how to put together a plan for tending to your four flowerpots. You will see that it's not necessary to fit **everything** in. Instead, I will invite you to include just the **essential** things that truly matter to you and add real value to your life. We want to let go of as much of the rest of it as we can.

Nurturing ourselves by keeping our flowerpots watered is powerful and effective because it's our way of taking care of ourselves holistically. Doing these important activities integrates our mind, body, and soul, thereby restoring us to wholeness. After all, feeling balanced doesn't come from setting boundaries or maintaining separation; it comes from feeling **whole.**

If we commit to incorporating our favorite things into our lives, we will derive energy from them. We will feel more alive. We'll also feel more creative and productive, more fun and loving. In general, everything will feel smoother and easier. When we find a way to proactively incorporate even a few small activities to satisfy these four aspects of ourselves, we can have a real shot at happiness, whether we're at work or off duty. This is a crucial part of our path to authentic success.

EXERCISES

LESSON 1:
SPIRIT

Learning and Growth

Goal: To look at the issues and challenges you face through the lens of spirituality, in order to promote your personal growth and learning.

Guidelines:

Anytime a stressful, confounding, and upsetting event occurs in your life, recognize that you have a rich learning opportunity available to you, if you choose to dig into it. Below are a few questions you might ask yourself to facilitate your process of discovery.

Before you begin, you'll want to take moment to connect with Spirit. You might do that by recalling a happy memory or thinking of a loved one, an activity that enlivens you, or a setting that brings you a sense of calm. Perhaps going for a walk in the woods, listening to a favorite song at full blast, or taking a minute to gaze at the sunset will do the trick. The idea is to do whatever it takes to elevate your perspective and remember that the crises or stressors that seem so pressing and urgent are, in fact, transient.

Questions to Ask Yourself:

1. Where does this experience fit into the broader picture of my life?

2. What is available for me to learn as a result of this situation?

3. If this experience were happening *for* me as a gift, what might that gift be?

4. Even though I don't like this experience, what byproduct do I receive from it? (For example, I get to be right, I get to be a victim, I get attention, I get to be seen as special.)

5. Am I willing to let go of that byproduct in exchange for releasing the negative pattern?

6. If I tune into my heart, what message does it have for me concerning this experience?

Co-creation

Goal: To cultivate your awareness of Spirit's presence and engage it in co-creative partnership.

Guidelines:

1. **Get clear** about your objectives. Do you have a specific goal you are trying to achieve? Is there a problem or issue you want to resolve?

2. **Articulate** your objective. You may silently reflect on it with focus and intention, verbalize it out loud, and/or write it down to reinforce your words. As you do this, you might imagine Spirit hearing and receiving your message.

3. **Envision** your wish and desires being manifested with grace and ease, then **release** them into the Universe.

4. **Pay attention** to your observations throughout the day. Treat any coincidences, synchronicities, and dreams with curiosity. Also make note of the results of your actions.

5. **Reflect** on what you observe. Consider what information may be pertinent and useful to your objectives. If any of the thoughts that come to you resonate with your gut, consider them clear guidance. Then determine your next steps. Remember, oftentimes the best action is none at all, particularly if you don't have strong

enough information to justify your desired action.

6. **Experiment** with acting upon your hunches. Continue to observe what happens, adjusting course as you go.

Notes:

- You'll know you're headed in the right direction when what you're doing feels good, when it feels right at a deep level. Feeling light, energetic, fully alive, and engaged is another indication that you're on the right path. Don't be surprised if your results seem to take shape seemingly by magic and if you keep receiving positive and encouraging feedback.

- Remember, co-creation is process of continual refinement, so stay open and keep learning from the feedback you receive as a result of your actions. If you're beating your head against a wall and not receiving encouragement, it might be a good time to reconsider your goals. On the other hand, if you're not getting positive feedback but still feel drawn to your goal, this may be a sign of how personally important it is to you. This is also valuable information that you may choose to interpret as internal encouragement.

- Sometimes you may receive messages or opportunities in an area that you haven't considered, or perhaps one that you believed wasn't of interest to you. You might even be presented opportunities that scare you. In cases like this, stay open to the possibility that this might be the Universe trying to show you your path.

LESSON 2:
TRUST

Goal: To develop a genuine sense of trust in Spirit and yourself.

Guidelines:

Use the events and situations in your life as opportunities to test the reliability of Spirit's guidance and your own intuition. As you engage in these experiments, you may want to begin with low-stakes situations. With practice, you will get more comfortable letting go of your attempts to control the details of your life using your old methods. As you do, you can begin to experiment with greater challenges. Eventually, you will witness for yourself how trust, openness, and receptivity can lead to better, more grace-filled outcomes. Here's what to do once you've identified your first experiment:

1. Take a few deep breaths to calm your mind and connect with both Spirit and your inner wisdom. If that feels like too much of a stretch, you might call to mind a mentor, teacher, or guru whom you consider wise.

2. Be quiet and still and listen for guidance from any of these sources.

3. If you're having trouble accessing it, take a few more deep breaths. You might try centering your awareness in either your heart or your third eye, and try again. Note: if nothing comes to you, you can try instead to emulate someone you admire who tends to take a different approach to things than you do.

4. Run your experiment.

5. Observe how it felt and what outcome resulted. If you're willing, take some extra time to journal about your experience. This will help deepen your learning and integrate it into your personal operating system. It will also help reinforce your successes.

6. Keep running the experiment with increasingly difficult challenges and observing the results. You'll see what opens up to you in your world.

LESSON 3:
ABUNDANCE

Goal: To cultivate a mindset that recognizes the abundance in your life.

Guidelines:

Cultivating a mindset of abundance will amplify your awareness of the blessings in your day-to-day life. Furthermore, it will create a strong foundation for you to draw upon when thoughts of scarcity creep into your mind.

1. Take a moment to contemplate the idea of abundance–that the Universe provides everything to all, and in myriad forms.

2. Anchoring yourself in that belief, expand your awareness and begin to look for evidence of abundance already present in your day-to-day life (e.g., the food you eat, your family, friendships, job, home, special talents).

3. If it's a struggle to come up with ideas, you might try one of these activities:

   • Take time to quiet your mind on a regular basis though a meditation or mindfulness practice, a walk around the block, a long shower, or whatever works for you.

   • Every morning for a month, write down in a journal one manifestation of abundance.

   • Reach out to a friend. Spending time with people you care about and who care about you will highlight the abundance of love and connection in your life. Your friend may also be able to help you brainstorm ways to attract what you are seeking.

   • Go out and do an activity you enjoy doing for its own sake. Being in the flow doing something you love may ignite your creativity in unexpected ways. It will also demonstrate the abundance of happiness and joy available to you.

   • If you're looking to validate the abundance of your own talents, begin to put yourself out into the world—especially if doing so scares you—and to open yourself up to what flows back to you as a result.

4. Notice how as soon as you start to appreciate what you already have, you begin to feel like you have more.

5. Be patient. Ideas often don't appear overnight, nor does money fall from the sky. Recognizing abundance is a process that builds with practice. And love can come knocking at your door; you just have to open the door to receive it. The key is to maintain hope and a positive attitude.

LESSON 4:
HUMILITY

<u>Goal</u>: To cultivate a humble attitude so that you can move forward more powerfully in your life. This specifically means becoming more comfortable accepting the following:

- Your limitations
- Your lack of importance relative to others
- What you cannot control
- Your discomfort in facing the unknown

<u>Guidelines:</u>

Below are suggestions of activities and questions to ask yourself that will assist you in working toward these goals.

1. Start by making a list of any one of the
   following:

   - Things you feel you are supposed to know
     but don't (i.e., knowledge, obstacles, or
     hang-ups you perceive as standing in your
     way). You can make this specific to a particu-
     lar objective. For example, perhaps you have
     your eye on a particular job listing, but the
     description mentions software familiarity you
     lack. Or perhaps you'd like to host a podcast,
     but you don't know the first thing about find-
     ing an audience or guests to interview. The
     idea here is to get specific about the partic-
     ular barriers in your way. This will help you
     make peace with your limitations and the un-
     known while also helping you see that it will
     be okay to ask for assistance.

   - Things you worry about frequently or are
     afraid of.

   - Things about you that you want to hide from
     others or aren't willing to admit to yourself.

   - Things you feel insecure about.

   - Things you expect of yourself that you don't
     feel you are fulfilling.

   - Things you find yourself constantly trying to
     prove to yourself and others.

   - Things that you feel others misjudge you for.

2. If you were to accept and value yourself unconditionally, regardless of what you wrote in response to the prompts above, what would it feel like to you? And what might you do differently in your life?

3. If you could buy into the notion that you are no more special or important than anyone else, how would your expectations change and how would your life be different?

4. If you were to fully embrace the idea that you are not *as* in control of the details of your life as you think, how might you loosen your grip on trying to get things to be exactly the way you think they should be? How would that feel to you?

5. Jot down examples of times in your life when something important turned out very differently from how you expected—and perhaps planned for. Reflect on what happened and how you felt about it. Did things turn out better or worse than you thought they would? What did you learn from the situation, and do you think the lesson was worthwhile?

6. Experiment with meditation. You can try any modality you like, whether it's guided meditation, loving-kindness meditation, mindfulness meditation, mantra meditation (such Transcendental Meditation), breathing meditation, or even group meditation or chanting. See what works for you.

Note:

If the word "meditation" itself feels like another thing you have to do—a **chore**—and creates much pressure for you, you may be holding too much of an expectation for what it "should" be. Release that expectation and any attachment to a particular outcome. All meditation entails is taking time to **pause** from any kind of "doing." Alternatively, if it's too uncomfortable for you to step out of your ceaseless "doing" mode, flip the words and think of this way: you are **doing** nothing. As long as you are sitting still and refraining from purposeful thinking or from trying to make progress on a task or goal, you are meditating. This should reduce the feeling of pressure and tee you up nicely to a productive day.

LESSON 5:
EGO AND SELF-WORTH

Ego

Goal: To learn to recognize when your ego has been activated and to reestablish the leadership of your wise inner guide.

Guidelines:

1. When you notice yourself being knocked off balance by unpleasant feelings such as anger, confusion, or self-doubt, take a moment to remind yourself that what's happened is your ego has just clocked in to work. It received a notification of a

potential threat, and it's ready to restore your comfort, safety, and control.

2. Try to identify what your ego is attempting to protect you from. Then ask yourself to evaluate honestly if the threat is real or imagined.

3. If there's real danger, identify specific action steps you can take to alleviate the problem. Write down your plan so you can get it out of your head. For danger that is only imagined, see if you can come up with another way to interpret the situation. Then make sure to thank your self-important ego for its vigilance and commitment to your safety. Flatter it by dispatching it back to its watchtower to monitor for actual threats.

4. If that doesn't help, simply acknowledge that you are experiencing discomfort, and then ask yourself if you can accept it. Can you get comfortable with being uncomfortable? Allow your experience of discomfort to be okay. Remember that it's just a feeling. And feelings are like visitors; they come and go. Recognize also that your discomfort is serving your learning and growth.

Self-Worth

Goal: To uncover hidden worthiness issues and restore your self-worth, confidence, and appreciation.

Guidelines:

- **Step 1: Cultivate awareness.** Reflect on the following questions as a starting point to help you discover your own personal worthiness hang-ups.

    1. If you close your eyes, can you remember a specific time when you received criticism and stewed about it? If so, what comments riled you? What were the circumstances around those comments? What misunderstandings, if any, did you feel were present?

    2. What were you repeatedly criticized for as a child? On the flip side, what kinds of qualities did you witness others being *praised* for?

    3. Were there any "bad raps" you were consistently given? Think about any qualities that you tend to reject in yourself, as well as unfair slights by others.

    4. What do you constantly find yourself trying to prove to yourself and others?

    5. What types of situations or comments tend to get your defenses up?

    6. When do you tend to compare yourself to others?

7. Who in your life drives you crazy? What about them is distasteful to you?

8. What are you afraid of asking for from others?

- **Step 2: Examine underlying beliefs.** If you want to take your new awareness a step further, consider examining any beliefs you hold about yourself that may reside beneath your answers to these questions.

- **Step 3: Reframe or update any that you now recognize as untrue.**

LESSON 6:
GRATITUDE

Goal: To cultivate a gratitude mindset and begin to witness how it shapes your life.

Guidelines:

There is a very specific exercise called a 32-Day Process, in which you commit to a behavior for thirty-two days in a row. Studies have shown that when it comes to cultivating a new mindset or habit, this window of time can help us make lasting change. Note that this doesn't have to be a time-consuming commitment. You can dedicate just a few minutes each day to the exercise. If you make it a small enough commitment (three to five minutes), it will be easier for you to stick with, even on your busiest, most hectic day.

1. Each day, write down one thing for which you are grateful. This may include **anything**, even something as small as your morning cup of coffee, a hug from your child, the smell of rain, a good laugh, or an interesting conversation. Or it could be something consistent in your life, perhaps something that works so smoothly you don't usually even think about it, like a rock-solid friendship you can always count on. The idea is to focus on something that has brought you comfort or joy, even if just momentarily.

2. Think about each item long enough to connect emotionally to it. Close your eyes and appreciate how it affects your life. Remember how it made you feel, perhaps focusing your attention on the place in your body where the emotion landed.

3. Continue this exercise daily for thirty-two days.

4. At the end of the time period, review what you've written and notice what feelings come up. Has the practice of being more cognizant of the blessings in your life helped you improve your overall outlook and mood?

Gratitude 2.0

Goal: To identify the learning available to you through difficult experiences.

<u>Guidelines:</u>

1. When you catch yourself telling the same story again and again about why you're upset, stop yourself. Close your eyes and take a few deep breaths as you center your awareness in your heart.

2. Once you feel calm, try to connect with your inner wise self and ask him/her for guidance to discover the lessons available to you. Here are examples of questions that might be helpful:

   - If this particular situation was put in place as a *gift* specifically for me, to help me learn an important lifelong lesson, what might that gift be?

   - What might this situation be reflecting back to me about how I treat myself or how I feel inside?

   - Assuming that I'm completely empowered in my own life, how might this situation actually be serving me?

3. Sit quietly, breathe into your heart, and listen for its message.

4. If answers don't pop up through simple reflection, consider buying a journal and spending time writing.

5. You may also consider posing questions to yourself out loud before bedtime so that they can marinate in your consciousness while you sleep. (If you're interested in taking it a step further, you might even pay attention to your dreams, as clues may show up there.)

Note:

- Sometimes answers will show up immediately, within the first minute or two. Other times it might take five minutes, twenty minutes, or even longer. Sometimes you'll need to make repeated attempts over weeks, months, or years, depending on how much practice you have with this. The importance of the issue and how entrenched it is in your life are also factors. We are given an entire lifetime to learn the essential lessons that each of our unique souls is here to learn. Be gentle with yourself and try not to get discouraged.

LESSON 7:
EMOTIONS

Goal: To release highly charged negative emotion in a way that's healthy and productive.

Guidelines for Stream-of-Consciousness Writing:

1. Gather a pen or pencil, some paper, and optionally, a candle; and go somewhere you won't be interrupted for at least twenty minutes. It's important for this exercise that you not use digital devices. The physical act of writing by hand can be more freeing and more activating than typing.

2. Take a moment to focus on the issue you are seeking to resolve. Candles can be helpful in diffusing negative energy, so if you'd like, light

your candle while setting your intention to allow your emotions to come up and out.

3. Begin writing, and continue without pausing for a minimum of twenty minutes. Your writing does not have be in complete sentences, in complete words, or even legible. You don't need to sound smart or make sense. The key is that during this time, you **do not** stop to collect your thoughts, as this needs to be an outlet for pure emotion.

4. Arm yourself with some phrases in case you draw a blank. Handy ones include:

   • "In this moment, I feel…"

   • "I'm angry because…"

   • "My life is unfair because…"

   • "I'm tired of this experience of…"

5. Give yourself permission to go with whatever comes out. If you're blocked, you can also write about that.

6. You'll know the task is complete when you feel an upward shift in your energy. You will feel empty as if the heaviness, sadness, or anger has just drained from your body.

7. When you are done, avoid rereading what you have written. In fact, it's best to destroy the paper, and the negativity contained within it, by burning or shredding it. If, however, there

is a valuable piece of insight from the exercise that you want to hold on to, you can preserve it however you wish.

8. Take a moment to acknowledge yourself for choosing to take the time to release your emotions in a healthy and productive way. If you feel better as a result, just notice that and make a mental note so that you may be more motivated to use this tool again the next time you need it.

LESSON 8:
RESPONSIBILITY

Goal: To fully own your emotional reactions in upsetting situations, identify your options, and get in the habit of responding productively and with a clear head.

Guidelines:

1. When you get upset, try to slow yourself down by taking a deep breath so you can refrain from reacting immediately. Instead of doing or saying anything, acknowledge the feeling going through you.

2. If you don't think you can stop yourself from blowing up and saying something that will aggravate the situation, remove yourself. Go find a safe place to express your emotions. If

the battle is between you and your thoughts, you can remind yourself to stop repeating your story in your head.

3. Give yourself space to become present with your true feelings. Allow yourself to cry out all your tears or scream into a pillow if you need to. You can also talk to a trusted friend, or journal, until you feel better. Afterward, take a moment to feel compassion for yourself and your experience.

4. Once you are calm, you can begin to determine how you want to respond. Questions you might ponder include:

   - Even though I perceive there to be something **wrong** with this situation, and even though I would like to respond by doing or saying [fill in the blank], what *other* options are possible?

   - If I could choose different thoughts about or interpretations of this situation, what might they be?

   - What interpretation of the situation would allow me to *feel* better?

   - What can I do or say that would be supportive to me and the situation right now?

5. Whatever you came up with, try it out and see how it goes. See if you are able to create a more productive and harmonious outcome.

Optional Advanced Step

I invite you to challenge yourself to not only take ownership of your emotional response but also use it for your personal growth and healing. When you're upset, you are probably rehashing a familiar story you've heard yourself tell countless times—all related to your past, fears about the future, or outdated beliefs. So, rather than blaming someone else for *causing* your problem, recognize that it's your own personal issue coming into play, and that you have an opportunity to use it to your benefit.

If you are willing to look into which specific hurts, fears, and judgments were triggered, you can update and reframe them in light of your current situation and the additional knowledge, experience, and wisdom you have gained in the years since the original event.

LESSON 9:
SELF-ADVOCACY

Goal: To support your needs and desires by speaking up and asking for what you want.

Guidelines:

1. Take a deep, centering breath and ask yourself, "If nothing I say or do could make me look bad, and it weren't a bother to anyone else, what would I want in this situation?"

2. If you aren't able to connect with a clear answer, ask yourself what is standing in your way. For example:

   - What is the fear? What perception of yourself are you attempting to manage?

- Is there someone you are trying to protect by not asking for what's good for you?

- What message or judgment is making what you want in your heart seem impossible or wrong?

- Who is that message coming from (a parent or grandparent, an authority figure, someone else from your past or present)?

3. Ask yourself again, reframing the question like this: What would I want if there were no "shoulds," expectations, or judgments of right, wrong, good, and bad?

4. Once you have clarity on what you want, let go of how other people might react, go ahead and ask for it, and see what happens.

5. If this is a skill you want to develop, begin taking the risk to ask for what you want in non-consequential situations, such as asking for the A/C to be turned up or down in a restaurant, or asking someone if they can do you a small favor. As you being to build confidence with small requests, you can gradually advance to more significant ones.

LESSON 10:
ACCEPTANCE

<u>Goals:</u>

1. To learn the skill of neutral observation and get better at letting go of judgments of good, bad, right, and wrong.

2. To release expectations of people and situations and allow for shortcomings in ourselves and others.

3. To create space and quiet to hear the small, wise voice inside us and experience compassion, appreciation, and gratitude.

Guidelines:

1. When you get triggered by life's events or by something someone has said or done, notice your feelings. But rather than getting carried away with your anger, sadness, or frustration, try instead to identify the *belief* that is being violated.

2. Remind yourself that things aren't inherently right or wrong, and that it's only our *thoughts* that define the situation that way.

3. Consult the wisdom of your heart for guidance about the situation and how you might view it with more neutrality. You might discover greater appreciation for the person or situation that has triggered you or connect with a feeling of love and compassion.

4. When times get really tough, try repeating this quote by Louise Hay: "All is well. Everything is working out for my highest good. Out of this situation only good will come. I am safe." For me, these words have proven very effective in providing temporary solace.

LESSON 11:
SELF-FORGIVENESS

Goal: To be less critical and to treat yourself with more kindness in the face of your perceived shortcomings and failures.

Guidelines:

1. When you catch yourself criticizing yourself over an attribute or behavior, stop immediately, and look for the judgment you are making about yourself. For example, you might be thinking something like *My kids never listen to me, and I'm always yelling at them. Everyone else's kids seem so well behaved. I must be a terrible parent.*

2. Once you've identified the judgment, express forgiveness toward yourself. This doesn't mean

forgiving yourself for being a terrible parent. You aren't one. Rather, forgive yourself for not yet knowing any better or for making a mistake—perhaps for not getting your child's attention in a way that worked. More important, forgive yourself if you have temporarily bought into any false belief about yourself or what the situation might mean about you personally. Remind yourself that every parent struggles at times with getting their kids to follow directions, and that we all lose our cool from time to time. For example, you might tell yourself any of the following:

- "I forgive myself for judging myself and my parenting so harshly."

- "I forgive myself for buying into the belief that losing my patience every now and then makes me a terrible parent."

- "I forgive myself for having failed to gain their compliance."

3. Then state your truth by reminding yourself of some fundamentals. For example: "The truth is I'm only human. I've got a lot on my plate, and sometimes I don't do the best job communicating with my kids. But that doesn't make me a terrible parent. In fact, I'm doing a great job under the circumstances. Overall, I'm working really hard and doing a great job managing everything going on."

4. If you're going through something truly difficult, offer yourself some compassion, just as you would for a friend who was struggling. Be kind to yourself!

5. Notice if your practice of self-forgiveness allows you to focus your energy in more productive ways.

LESSON 12:
INTENTIONS

Goal: To use the practice of setting intentions to help you accomplish something important to you.

Guidelines:

Whether you're thinking about a project or challenge or the way you'd like to experience an upcoming event, follow these guidelines for setting your intentions. As an aside, remember that intentions can serve you well for small goals (e.g., smiling more often or taking the time periodically to tell your husband how handsome he is), long-term projects (e.g., coaching your first season of soccer or writing a children's book), or one-time events or activities (e.g., hosting Thanksgiving dinner or going on a first date).

1. Close your eyes and ask yourself, "What is the *outcome* I wish to produce?"

2. When you have a clear idea of what it is, take a moment to let it really sink in. Remember, the clearer you are in visualizing and stating what you desire, the better your instructions to the Universe are and the more likely your wishes will be manifested. To promote greater clarity, you might consider writing them down or saying them out loud to yourself or a friend.

3. Set your intention free and stay open to receiving *whatever* may come forward. Trust that what comes forward will be for your highest good.

Notes:

- Remember to frame intentions in a positive way ("I want to do X") as opposed to a negative way ("I don't want to do Y"). Someone going through a divorce might say, "My goal is to stop stewing about my ex-husband." The way to express this as an intention might be "My intention is to let go of thoughts that don't serve me."

- The practice of setting intentions also applies to how we experience our lives. So, for example, you may ask yourself, "What is the *experience* I wish to have in the process of moving toward my desired outcome?" I strongly encourage you to write down such intentions, because when we get busy and preoccupied with daily tasks, it is easy to forget to make our experience—how we *feel* as we pursue our goals—as important as the outcome. When we write our intentions down, we have something to refer back to if we wish to remain accountable for how we're **being** during the course of our **doing.** This is what determines how much pain and suffering we can sidestep and how much joy we can attract into our experiences.

- For longer-term projects and challenges, I recommend revisiting and updating your intentions periodically to reflect new insights and incorporate new developments. This will help keep what you desire to manifest—and the way you want to feel along the way—front and center in your consciousness.

LESSON 13:
MIND-BODY PARTNERSHIP

Goal: To establish strong communication and partnership between your mind and your body.

Guidelines:

1. When you feel any pain or fatigue in your body, large or small, take a moment to acknowledge its presence.

2. Ask yourself what it is trying to communicate to you. (If you're willing to personify the pain, you can address your question directly to Pain itself.)

3. Once you've heard the message, assess the situation and determine your next steps. These

may be as simple as stretching or taking a nap, a bath, or a short walk around the block. You may want to schedule a massage or visit your doctor, chiropractor, acupuncturist, or other healer. Perhaps the exercise program you've been following is causing problems, and you need to take a break. Maybe you should start eating a healthier diet or drinking more water. Your body will let you know what it needs.

4. Continue to listen to what your body needs, and respond to it promptly, before it needs to cause even greater pain just to get your attention.

LESSON 14:

THE MYTH OF "WORK-LIFE BALANCE"

Goal: To increase the possibility of feeling happy, fulfilled, and whole by nurturing yourself holistically on the physical, mental, emotional, and spiritual levels.

Guidelines:

Follow these instructions (based on an assignment Ron and Mary Hulnick gave me and my classmates in our master's program) to set up a system of accountability for nurturing your mind, body, and soul.

1. Make a chart like the one below, using paper, a spreadsheet program, or one of the many habit-building mobile apps.

FOUR FLOWERPOTS TRACKING WORKSHEET

SPIRITUAL	EMOTIONAL	MENTAL	PHYSICAL	
				Activity
				M
				T
				W
				Th
				F
				S
				S
				Summary
				M
				T
				W
				Th
				F
				S
				S
				Summary
				M
				T
				W
				Th
				F
				S
				S
				Summary
				M
				T
				W
				Th
				F
				S
				S
				Summary

2. Within each category (Physical, Mental, Emotional, and Spiritual), fill in three to five activities that you know will bring you joy. Include the minimum number of times per week that you'd like to do each one. (Note: creating this chart need not take more than about ten minutes.)

3. Every evening for the next four weeks, take a couple of minutes to go down the list and check off the activities you accomplished that day. This is also a good time to double-check for activities that you intended to complete but haven't, and to do them before the day is done.

4. At the end of the month, when you've completed the whole chart, take a few minutes to look back and reflect on how you felt over the course of the month. Did you feel happier, more energetic, joyful, and alive?

5. Repeat for a second, third, and fourth month... or forever.

Notes:

- The list you come up with is highly individual and is not intended to include large, difficult, or time-consuming activities. It's also not about grand, life-changing adventures. Rather, it should include the types of things that you know from your own life experience (or from your heart's desire) that you can count on to give you a burst of energy and create joy. This is about reflecting on what you know *already* makes you happy.

- The activities you select can be quite simple—for example, starting your morning with a glass of lemon water, writing a daily affirmation, throwing out one thing a day, or taking one minute each day to think of something for which you feel grateful. Other activities might be more time-consuming—for example, exercising, spending time reading, or reaching out to a friend. Because activities like these do take more than just a couple of minutes, they're easier to put off, and that's why an action plan and tracker like this is so effective. It helps build accountability—and may eventually give rise to an automatic habit.

- If find yourself avoiding certain activities, or if you find them burdensome, consider that a clue. Perhaps the activity isn't aligned with your heart's desire. These activities should definitely feel good. To reiterate: this is about self-*nurturance*—not what you *should* do, but rather what you can count on to bring you joy.

Remember: Nurturing ourselves is what energizes us. It helps us reconnect with our purpose. When our flowerpots are watered, it becomes easier to accomplish what we want to accomplish, and along the way, we get to have the quality of experience we wish for ourselves. When our experience of life is not going this way, it's a sign that we need to recenter ourselves. We need to reconnect with the wise one inside as we reassess and recalibrate the most important priorities in our lives and make sure they're all represented.

ACKNOWLEDGMENTS

I'd like to acknowledge the following people for their roles in assisting me in bringing this project to completion. First and foremost, Ron and Mary Hulnick for introducing these concepts to me, designing the spiritual psychology curriculum the way they did, and setting the stage for the experiences that helped infuse these lessons into my way of being.

I'm also grateful to all of my facilitators, clients, and courageously vulnerable classmates for sharing their hearts and minds with me and further supporting me in my learning journey. I especially want to acknowledge my project teammates, Elaine Lipworth, Jesse Gros, and Steven Starr. They lovingly shined a light on my blind spots and pointed me in the direction of the specific work I needed to focus on within myself to become more calm, balanced, centered, and whole, and ultimately become the person I wanted to become.

I'm grateful for Marc, who was by my side every step of the way—from our hike through Temescal Canyon in 2013 where we came up with the seedlings of this book to putting up with all my weekends away from the family, listening to all my gripes during the challenging parts of the process, and finally, sitting with me at Bagel Nosh to work on the final edits to bring this book across the finish line in 2020. His patience and emotional support along the way were the ingredients that allowed me to bring this project to fruition.

My children were also an incredibly important part of this project. Cooper inspired so much of my work in the early days, and Hannah Grace brought new opportunities for the lessons to take an even deeper hold within my being. Also, I appreciate my parents for their openness while I pursued a program they didn't understand, and my mom for being my first editor.

I'm grateful to my very first coach, Jane Cruz, who made me feel safe enough to share all of my deepest fears and insecurities openly. My thanks also go out to Carlee Chiate, Carrie Johnson, Kahli Small, and Nili Hudson for their ongoing interest, support, and encouragement in pursuing this project. Rena Garland, Lori Richards, Shelly and Ptolemy Slocum, and Vicki Falcone deserve a special thank you for giving me encouragement during my darkest times, when I felt like this project was taking way too long.

I also want to give a shout-out to my very first readers: my sister-in-law Tricia Campbell, Hank Peck, Joanne Cantor, Grace Shu, Dawn Urbont, Elyse Meshnick, Karen Hallo, Andrea Crow, Jeff Rosin, Eileen Fraser, Tracy Poff, Linda Lu, Kenny and Anya Davis, Ratana Therakulsathit, Yassie Entekhabit, Neha Prassad, Jennifer Hui, Renae Hwang, Adam Scott, Monica Ciociola, Cindy Codispoti Parker, and Liz Hanrahan, and one other person who was kind enough to give me feedback but left their name out so I never could thank him or her personally.

A gigantic thank you goes to Suzanne Potts, Maya Lang, and Hilary Roberts for taking me on as a client, providing suggestions and guidance, and showing me how to make my manuscript shine.

And finally, I'm grateful to the Universal field of Intelligence that made this all possible.

DID YOU ENJOY THIS BOOK?

If you enjoyed this book, please visit alisoncampbellcoaching. com, where you can inquire about workshops, speaking engagements, or bulk orders of this book, or sign up to receive my occasional newsletter and information about upcoming events.

If you benefited from reading this book, please tell me your story. Taking the time to share your experiences will help you reinforce your learning, and I would be so grateful to know how these lessons are making a difference in my readers' lives. Please feel free to reach out to me directly at AliCCoaching@gmail.com.

You can purchase additional copies of this book at alisoncampbellcoaching.com or store.vervante.com/c/v/bookstore.html